Mary

Please Believe me.

Caring
FOR THE Soul

CWR Waverley Abbey House, Waverley Lane, Farnham, Surrey GU9 8EP

Unless otherwise indicated, Scripture quotations are taken from *The Holy Bible*, New International Version © 1984, International Bible Society. Other versions used include:
The Holy Bible, New King James Version (NKJV) © 1982, Thomas Nelson, Inc.;
The New American Standard Bible (NASB) © 1997, Foundation Publications;
The Amplified Bible (AMP) © 1987, Zondervan Publishing House;
The Holy Bible, King James Version (KJV) © 1977, Thomas Nelson, Inc;
The Holy Bible, New Revised Standard Version (NRSV) © 1989, Thomas Nelson, Inc;
The New Testament in Modern English, revised edition (PHILLIPS) © 1958, 1960, JB Phillips;
The Bible. A New Translation (MOFFAT) © 1950, 1952, 1953, 1954, James AR Moffatt.
The Holy Bible, Authorised Version (AV) © 1611, 1982, Trinitarian Bible Society.

CARING FOR THE SOUL
A compilation of excerpts from *Every Day with Jesus*
by Selwyn Hughes 1988, 1993, 1995, 1996, 1997, 1999.
Edited by Monica de Vries
© CWR 2005

Concept development, editing, design and production by
Struik Christian Books
A division of New Holland Publishing (South Africa) (Pty) Ltd
(New Holland Publishing is a member of Johnnic Communications Ltd)
Cornelis Struik House
80 McKenzie Street
Cape Town 8001

Reg. No. 1971/009721/07

DTP by Louise Fouché
Cover design by Joleen Coetzee
Cover photograph by Photo Access
Reproduced, printed and bound in Singapore

ISBN 1 85345 346 3

SELWYN HUGHES

Caring
FOR THE *Soul*

The way to inner serenity

Quiet time

The pastor prayed eloquently,
'Father, we thank You for
moments of quietness.'
Forgive my ignorance, Lord,
but what and when is quietness?
Oh, of course. It's the time the organ
plays softly and people cough and babies fuss.
No? It's probably when the washing machine
finally stops and the television blows a tube.
No? Maybe it's when I sleep and only
the quiet noise of dreams scamper across my mind.
No again? Then it must be when I'm
alone in the hills with only the chirp
of birds and rustle of wind.
'No, my child, it's when you are alone
with Me in the middle of life's
raucous insanity.'

IN GOD'S GYMNASIUM

FOR READING & MEDITATION – 1 TIMOTHY 4:1–16

... train yourself to be godly. (v 7)

To get rid of spiritual flabbiness and fat, to be lean and fit spiritually should be the aim of every one of Christ's disciples.

How do we keep our physical bodies in trim? To lose excess weight it is helpful to do more than dieting. One should engage in physical exercise as well – jogging, weight lifting, etc. As physical exercises increase the body's fitness and health, so spiritual exercises improve spiritual fitness and vitality.

I am therefore inviting you to start a spiritual exercise programme that will result in your being spiritually fitter than ever before. Clearly, as our text for today makes plain, godliness does not just happen. We have to *train* ourselves for it. The challenge facing us is to 'prepare for a workout'. There is no other way to find health for the soul.

O Father, help me rise to this challenge. I want to be fitter than ever to carry out your purposes. May all spiritual flabbiness, all excess spiritual weight be trimmed by exercising my soul. In Jesus' Name. Amen.

RIGHT ACTS – WRONG MOTIVES

For reading & meditation – 1 Corinthians 15:1–11

But by the grace of God I am what I am ... (v 10)

To regard disciplined self-advancing as the secret of becoming a godly person is an error since it is possible to do right but for the wrong reason.

Many Christians practise disciplines to advance themselves. They depend more on their spiritual exercises for progress in godliness than on the grace of God. This is the worst kind of legalism. The apostle Paul was one of the most disciplined disciples in history, yet he gave the credit for his spiritual progress to the grace of God: 'By the grace of God I am what I am'.

We must guard against the tendency to place greater emphasis on what we do for God than on what He has done for us. I regularly ask students who are training: Where is your dependency? The more we learn and understand, the more likely it is that we will depend on our knowledge rather than the grace of God.

JANUARY 2 | The care of the soul

Father, may I totally depend on You. By grace I was saved, and by grace I am sustained. Thank You, my Father. Amen.

DEPENDABLE DISCIPLES

FOR READING & MEDITATION – GALATIANS 5:1–15

... do not use your freedom to indulge the sinful nature ... (v 13)

Some Christians shy away from the word 'discipline' because it smacks of lack of freedom and harsh rituals. Where there is no discipline there are no dependable disciples.

The gift of grace is a blessed privilege but our lives have to be permeated with discipline too. A woman suffering from paralysis of the legs went to a healing service in her Anglican church and was instantly made better. A few days later she said, 'Lord, you have healed me of paralysis of the legs. What are You going to do about my overweight?' The answer seemed to come as she opened up her Bible and read: 'This kind goeth not out but by prayer and fasting' (Matt 17:21 AV). Where only dependence could bring results, that was the answer. Where only discipline could bring results, that was the answer.

The effective Christian life is a balanced life. Dependence plus discipline makes dependable disciples.

The care of the soul

🕊 *My Father and my God, You are showing me too my need for discipline. May I also accept that – wholeheartedly. In Jesus' Name. Amen.*

DISCIPLINE WITHOUT DIRECTION

FOR READING & MEDITATION – ROMANS 8:28–39
For those God foreknew he also predestined to be
conformed to the likeness of his Son ... (v 29)

When it comes to discipline in the Christian life many believers feel that practice is tiresome and tedious. But how different when we see the direction in which discipline takes us. God's great goal for us is to make us like Christ. We are predestined for that – God's grace is working in our lives to make us more like Christ.

But if we are predestined to be conformed to Christ's image, what need is there of discipline? Because it is through discipline that we assent to God's purposes for our lives. Spiritual discipline puts us in a position where we will receive the grace that flows from the heart of our Saviour. CH Spurgeon said: 'I must take care above all that I cultivate communion with Christ, for though that can never be the basis for my peace ... it will be the channel of it.'

🐾 *O Father, your biggest single purpose for my life is to make me like Jesus. You will do your part, help me do mine. Amen.*

LOVE THAT 'SPRINGS'

FOR READING & MEDITATION – 1 TIMOTHY 1:1–11

The goal of this command is love, which comes from
a pure heart and a good conscience and a sincere faith. (v 5)

We don't usually connect discipline with spontaneity, but the
apostle Paul seems to be doing this in this text. Discipline
produces a love that 'springs', he says.

The goal of Christian discipline is to make us like Jesus. We are
predestined to be conformed to his image. Has there ever been
anyone more disciplined and yet more free than Jesus? The true
Christian says, 'I am free to do as I ought.' Liberty comes from
obedience to law. That is the way life works.

Love can be spontaneous and free only as it comes from a life
that has discipline. Any supposed freedom leaves you with a love
that sighs and soon dies. A disciplined person has a love that
springs – and a love that sings.

*Father, help me grasp the fact that freedom and discipline are
not mutually exclusive. I am free not to do as I like but to do as I
ought. Drive this truth deep into my spirit I pray. In Christ's Name.
Amen.*

GOD'S ONLY PUBLISHED WORK

FOR READING & MEDITATION – 2 TIMOTHY 3:12–17
All Scripture is God-breathed and is useful for teaching,
rebuking, correcting and training in righteousness ... (v 16)

Godly people are *disciplined* people; so were heroes of Christian history. I have never known a man or woman who evidenced a high degree of spiritual fitness who was not disciplined.

One of the first things we must discipline ourselves to do if we are to train ourselves for godliness is have a regular intake from the Word of God. The Bible is God's one and only published work, the only book that has upon it the stamp of divine infallibility. Would you like to know who God is and how to live a life that pleases the Lord?

If we are to know God and train ourselves for godliness we must dip into the Word of God frequently. The number of committed Christians who spend time studying the Bible daily, or even regularly, is astonishingly low.

Father, help me become more deeply convinced of the importance of exposing my soul to your Word regularly. May your Word be my 'necessary food'. In Jesus' Name. Amen.

HEARING THE WORD OF GOD

FOR READING & MEDITATION – 1 TIMOTHY 4:1–16

Until I come, devote yourself to the public reading
of Scripture, to preaching and to teaching. (v 14)

In many Christian meetings or services little or no place is given to
the public reading of the Scriptures. I have been in several
churches recently where there was a great deal of music, singing
and worship, but not once were the congregation asked to remain
silent and listen to the reading of the Word of God.

Romans 10 says: 'Faith comes from hearing the message, and the
message is heard through the word of Christ' (v 17). Paul is empha-
sising the need to preach and teach God's message. Many a time as
I have listened to the Bible being read in church I have picked up
something I had missed in my personal reading of the Scriptures.

It is important for God's people to sing, praise and worship Him
but also to hear his Word.

The care of the soul

JANUARY 7

*O Father, awaken your Church to the importance of publicly
reading your Word – the Word that is greater than men's words. Help
us give it its rightful place in our midst. In Christ's Name. Amen.*

READING THE BIBLE

For reading & meditation – Matthew 4:1–11

Man does not live on bread alone, but on every word
that comes from the mouth of God. (v 4)

The daily or regular intake of the Scriptures is not only 'the first
exercise of the soul'; it is also the broadest. If you want to become more like Jesus and reflect his character then discipline yourself to read the Scriptures.

John Blanchard writes in his book *How to Enjoy the Bible:*
'Surely we have to be realistic and honest with ourselves to know
how regularly we need to turn to the Bible. How often do we face
problems, temptations and pressures? *Every day!* How often do
we need instruction, guidance and greater encouragement? *Every
day!* How often do we need to hear God's voice, feel his touch,
know his power? The answer to all these questions is the same:
every day!'

🖎 *Father, I see I have to draw on your boundless store of grace,
some of which comes to me only as I read your Word, from hour
by hour and day by day. I see this but help me live by it. In Christ's
Name I pray. Amen.*

EVERY DAY WITH JESUS

FOR READING & MEDITATION – ACTS 17:1–15

Now the Bereans were of more noble character ...
for they ... examined the Scriptures every day ... (v 11)

Hearing and reading the Word of God are important and effective spiritual exercises. So also is studying it.

Paul and Silas, having provoked the Jews at Thessalonica were forced to flee to save their lives. They escaped to Berea. The Bereans 'were of more noble character, for they ... examined the Scriptures every day to see if what Paul said was true'.

The more you study the Bible the more you will grow. When the apostle Paul was languishing in prison and anticipating the arrival of his young friend Timothy he said: 'When you come, bring the cloak ... especially the parchments' (2 Tim 4:13). In cold and miserable conditions the apostle asked for two things: something for his body and something for his soul. Paul still wanted to delve into the Word of God until the day he died.

O Father, give me the same desire that Paul had: to delve into your Word and explore its mysteries and wonders. Help me discipline myself. In Jesus' Name. Amen.

READ LESS – MEDITATE MORE

FOR READING & MEDITATION – PSALM 39:1–13

My heart grew hot within me,
and as I meditated, the fire burned ... (v 3)

No principle of Scripture is more important than that of meditating on what God has written in the Bible.

One of the tragedies of our day is that meditation is linked more to non-Christian systems of belief than with Biblical Christianity, but there is a vast difference. Meditation is deep focused thinking. Only about one per cent of Christians engage in this spiritual exercise.

Meditation acts like bellows on a little flame and transforms it into a blazing fire. A Puritan pastor said: 'The reason we come away so cold from reading the Word is because we do not warm ourselves at the fire of meditation.' Here's one of the most helpful pieces of advice I can give: Read less and meditate more.

Father, I love your Word. I love to read it daily, but forgive me that I fail to meditate on it enough. Help me to re-establish my priorities so that I give less time to other matters and more to this. In Christ's Name. Amen.

REGULAR RESPIRATION

FOR READING & MEDITATION – LUKE 18:1–8

Then Jesus told his disciples a parable to show them
that they should always pray and not give up. (v 1)

Some would name prayer as the first spiritual exercise, but that
is not my opinion.

We read that the first Christians devoted themselves to (1) the
apostles' teaching, (2) the fellowship, (3) the breaking of bread,
(4) prayer (Acts 2:42).

One of the major reasons for lack of godliness is prayerlessness.
A tiger's first objective when it attacks another animal is to slit its
throat with its sharp claws. When the animal is no longer able to
breathe it is finished. Satan, the enemy of our souls, follows this
same strategy in his attack on us. If he can stop us breathing
spiritually by preventing us from praying, then we become powerless and a plaything in his hands.

Whatever you do and however many Christian meetings you
attend there can be no advance towards godliness unless you give
time to prayer.

*Gracious Father, help me to give no place to the devil, es-
pecially in this matter of prayer. May I constantly replenish my
spiritual life through prayer. In Jesus' Name. Amen.*

GOD'S 'VLE'

FOR READING & MEDITATION – JEREMIAH 33:1–9
Call to me and I will answer you and tell you great
and unsearchable things you do not know. (v 3)

God delights in talking to us – our text for today makes that clear. But how eager are we to talk to Him?

A television programme reported on the setting up of a large radio receiver in New Mexico, designed to pick up any signals from life-forms in outer space.

It has been named the 'VLE – Very Large Ear'. I wonder how many of those scientists realise that a word has already come to us from the heavenly realm – a Word made flesh in the Person of God's Son. But not only has God spoken to us in Christ; He has made it possible for us to speak to Him. And that ear, I might add, is continually open to us.

Father, I do not wonder for I have often gone to my knees feeling defeated and have risen again victorious. I am more grateful than I can say for the privilege of being able to talk to You in prayer. Thank You my Father. Amen.

CHRIST EXPECTS US TO PRAY

FOR READING & MEDITATION – LUKE 11:1–13

He said to them, 'When you pray, say:
"Father, hallowed be your name ..."' (v 2)

Whether or not we think prayer is a good idea is irrelevant – Christ expects us to pray. When we become Christians, we bring our lives under the authority of Christ and submit to his commands. And one of his commands is that we should always pray (Luke 18:1). This is not intended to be hurtful, but I believe, that a Christian who doesn't pray is being insubordinate. Prayerlessness is in effect reacting to Christ's statement, 'You should always pray' with the attitude, 'I don't care what You say, I am not going to do it'.

Well, what He has said in his Word about prayer conveys his will for you as strongly as if He appeared to you in your room and spoke to you personally.

Gracious Father, help me not to wriggle when I am cornered like this. You challenge me in order to change me. Help me deepen my prayer life and expand my times of communion with You. In the Saviour's Name I pray. Amen.

EVERY PRAYER ANSWERED

FOR READING & MEDITATION – ISAIAH 65:17–25

Before they call I will answer; while they
are still speaking I will hear ... (v 24)

If prayer is of such prime importance why do we pray so little?
One reason is lack of discipline. Prayer is not planned.

For some people another reason may be doubt if anything happens as a result of prayer. Prayer is not like putting money in a slot machine and getting immediate results. Sometimes the results are instant but more commonly they are not. Many times prayer is answered in a way that we human beings cannot see or understand. Be assured of this: God hears and answers every prayer.

Another reason why we do not pray more is because of self-sufficiency. Many reading these words will have received a fairly good education, maybe even acquired a degree. As a consequence life seems manageable. Jesus said: 'Apart from me you can do nothing' (John 15:5). Nothing really matters unless He is in it. And if He isn't then it doesn't really matter at all.

🖎 *Give me the mind to pray, the will to pray and the love to pray. In Jesus' Name. Amen.*

AN IMPORTANT SECRET

FOR READING & MEDITATION – PHILIPPIANS 4:1–9

... in everything, by prayer and petition, with thanksgiving,
present your requests to God. (v 6)

The secret is to begin your prayer time with meditation. I learned this many years ago from the writings of George Muller. 'For the first ten years of my Christian life, my habit was to wash and dress myself, then turn to prayer.' But often he felt his prayer time was tedious and boring. Then, as he changed his approach to prayer by first reading the Word of God and meditating on it. He would speak to God about the things he had discovered in the Word and never again did he find prayer wearisome.

Our Lord prayed much. Do you want to be like Him? Then discipline yourself to be a person of prayer. One thing is sure: after hearing, reading and studying God's Word, prayer is the next most important spiritual exercise.

Gracious Father, I cannot pray as I ought unless your Spirit inspires me, so that I may more and more pray according to your will. I would live a Spirit-inspired life hence a Spirit-empowered life. In Jesus' Name. Amen.

'WORTH-SHIP'

FOR READING & MEDITATION – REVELATION 4:1–11
'You are worthy, our Lord and God,
to receive glory and honour and power ...' (v 11)

Worship is 'the response of a heart in love with God', but how does the heart become filled with love for God? We can focus the soul's attention on God, his attributes and character. The more we focus on God the more responsive we become to Him, and the more responsive we become to Him the more godly we become.

But what really is worship? How can it be understood? And how different is it from prayer and praise? The word *worship* comes from the Saxon word *weorthscype* which later became 'worthship'. Nowadays we simply say *worship*. So worship is ascribing proper worth to God, exalting Him and regarding Him as being deserving of adoration and honour. Notice how the twenty-four elders laid their crowns before the throne and cried: 'You are *worthy* ...' The soul knows nothing of worship unless it has a deep understanding of the Almighty's intrinsic worth.

O God, my soul was made to worship. Teach me how to worship You with all my heart. In Jesus' Name. Amen.

IN AWE OF GOD

For reading & meditation – Job 42:1–6

'My ears had heard of you but
now my eyes have seen you.' (v 5)

Have you noticed how infrequently the word *awe* is used now-adays? I heard British psychiatrist, Dr Anthony Claire, say: 'This present generation seems to have lost its sense of awe.'

It is probably right to assume that most believers know how to pray and praise, but how often do we stand in awe before God? Job developed a sense of awe as a result of God's dealings with him. Daniel, responded in a similar way. After God had addressed him he said: 'I stood up trembling' (Dan 10:11).

Do we ever tremble before God? I would go so far as to say that we will never be able to truly convey to others what God means to us unless we know what it is to stand in awe before Him and tremble at his glory.

O God, I love You, praise You, and pray to You, but am I in awe of You? Grant that my familiarity with You will not blunt my need to see You as an awesome God. Amen.

WORSHIP – GOD'S RIGHT

FOR READING & MEDITATION – 1 CHRONICLES 16:7–36

For great is the LORD and most worthy of praise;
he is to be feared above all gods. (v 25)

Worship is focusing on the greatness, the glory and the supreme worth of God and responding to Him in adoration and awe.

CS Lewis: 'What do we mean when we say that a picture is 'admirable'? The sense in which the picture 'deserves' or 'demands' admiration is this; admiration is the correct, adequate, or appropriate response to it, and if we do not admire we shall be great losers, we shall have missed something.'

All right-minded people respond to beauty with admiration and awe. Just as a glorious sunset evokes a spontaneous response, so the soul cannot encounter the worthiness of God without responding in true worship. If you could catch a glimpse of how worthy God is, how beautiful his character, how glorious his nature, you would fall on your face and worship Him.

O Father, help me contemplate your glory in such a way that I will be humbled and fall in awe before You. This I ask in the Saviour's peerless and precious Name. Amen.

The care of the soul

IN SPIRIT AND IN TRUTH

For reading & meditation – Philippians 3:1–11
For it is we who ... worship by the Spirit of God ... (v 3)

God reveals Himself to us in many different ways. Creation is just one of them. Who hasn't been thrilled at some aspect of creation and thought: Only a great and mighty God could have made this?

God has made Himself known to us also through the Person of his Son, the Lord Jesus Christ. God reveals Himself to us through his Word. As we read the Scriptures the Holy Spirit opens the eyes of our understanding and what we see of God causes our soul to respond to Him in adoration.

We worship 'in spirit and in truth' (John 4:24) when we have the Spirit of God within us and live our lives according to the truth contained in the Scriptures. That is why meditation on God's Word is an essential prerequisite not only for prayer but also for worship. Worship reaches its highest point when God is being contemplated.

The care of the soul

God my Father, You are teaching me how to pray; teach me also how to worship. In Jesus' Name. Amen.

PRAISE AND WORSHIP

FOR READING & MEDITATION – PSALM 48:1–14

Within your temple, O God,
we meditate on your unfailing love. (v 9)

Prayer involves talking to God and God talking to you. Praise is thanking God for the things He has done, is doing, and is going to do. Worship is adoring God not so much for what He does but for who He is. I focus on attributes such as love, holiness, righteousness, power, grace. And as I meditate the fire burns and my soul soars in adoration of God.

Some Christians think of worship as something they do only on Sundays when they meet with other Christians in church. This is a false view of worship. AW Tozer said: 'If you will not worship God seven days a week you do not worship Him on one day a week.' Corporate worship must never be a substitute for individual worship. The great saints of the past would all agree that training ourselves to worship leads to increased godliness.

Thank You my Father. I see that worship is different from praise and different from thanksgiving. Help me to enter more keenly into the exercise of worship. Amen.

OPEN-DOORED TO GOD

For reading & meditation – Luke 4:38–44

At daybreak Jesus went out to a solitary place. (v 42)

The next exercise is seeking solitude. Extroverts will find this exercise difficult. However, even if you are an extrovert I would urge you to consider its benefits.

Seeking solitude involves temporarily withdrawing from activity and finding a quiet or private place in order to rest, relax and give oneself to spiritual purposes. It is this giving of oneself to spiritual purposes that differentiates seeking seclusion from having a day out or a brief holiday.

Our Lord often sought solitude. He healed various kinds of sickness and cast demons out of many people. Crowds flocked to Him for spiritual and physical help. But after all this activity we read: Jesus 'went out to a solitary place'. At that moment it was more important to discipline Himself to be alone than to continue healing the sick and casting out demons. Involvement with people and ministry to others is important, but so also is solitude. The art is to know which of these is the priority of the moment.

The care of the soul

Father, teach me how to prioritise. In Christ's Name I pray. Amen.

ISLANDS OF SOLITUDE

Be silent before the Sovereign Lord,
for the day of the Lord is near. (v 7)

'Many of the ills of life,' said Blaise Pascal, in the seventeenth century, 'come from not being able to sit in a room – alone.' I wonder what he would say were he alive now. A large section of the population today, especially the young, seem afraid of being alone. Jean Fleming observed: ' We have become a people with an aversion to quiet and an uneasiness with being alone.' Those who do not have 'islands of solitude' soon become frantic personalities. Kenneth Fearing says of such people:

> And wow they died as wow they lived,
> Going zoom to the office, and whoosh home to sleep.

The solitude I am talking about is using seclusion for spiritual purposes, not just to be quiet but to 'be silent before the Sovereign Lord'. That is the reason Jesus found solitude essential. It may be helpful to find a tranquil spot away from noise and other people.

 O God my Father, help me to find an 'island of solitude'. I see the value of doing so. Amen.

NOT ENOUGH SILENCE

For reading & meditation – 1 Kings 19:9–18

And after the fire came a gentle whisper. (v 12)

What is the real point of exercising the soul through solitude? The primary purpose is to hear the voice of God more clearly and to equip ourselves to be of better service to others. The Bible fairly bulges with accounts of men and women who had a daily appointment with God yet felt it necessary to find solitude at times in order to hear his voice more clearly. I think of Habbakuk standing at his guard-post, waiting to hear what God would say to him (Hab 2:1). I think of Paul making his way into the deserts of Arabia to rethink his theology (Gal 1:17). Then we see Elijah having a spiritual *tête-à-tête* with the Almighty and hearing the gentle whisper of his voice.

This is not to say that we have to be alone to hear God's voice. But sometimes we need a time of solitude.

The care of the soul

JANUARY 23

Lord Jesus Christ, You needed solitude to hear your Father's voice and discover his will. Help me to add time for solitude to my spiritual workout. In Jesus' Name. Amen.

DEEPENED UNDERSTANDING

FOR READING & MEDITATION – MATTHEW 26:36–46

[Jesus] said to them, 'Sit here while
I go over there and pray.' (v 36)

Dietrich Bonhoeffer, in his book *Life Together*, wrote: 'One
who wants fellowship without solitude plunges into the void
of words and feelings, and one who seeks solitude without fellowship perishes in the abyss of vanity, self-infatuation and despair.'

If we want to be like Jesus – and that, after all, is the purpose
of every one of the spiritual disciplines – then we must get away
from people so that we will have more to offer when we are with
others. Solitude deepens our understanding of people, gives us a
new freedom from our own concerns and heightens our sensitiv-
ity towards them.

We are better able to give ourselves to others after giving ourselves to God during times of solitude. If you are saying to yourself
now, 'This makes sense but I'm too busy,' then I would reply that
the busier you are the greater your need of solitude.

*O Father, I need your help in organising my life so that spiritu-
al exercises take priority over other things. In Jesus' Name. Amen.*

SETTLING DOWN IN GOD

FOR READING & MEDITATION – 1 KINGS 6:1–13

... no hammer, chisel or any other iron tool was
heard at the temple site while it was being built. (v 7)

We – as temples of the Holy Spirit – need to be built up through
times of quietness. Plan such times for the year ahead.

All the great men and women of God have been disciplined
people. And their discipline included finding time for solitude. I
realise that mothers with families for example – will find it almost
impossible to have an extended period of solitude.

Susannah Wesley, mother of John and Charles Wesley, had a
very large family, and although she longed for times when she
could be alone with God she found it difficult. So when she needed
solitude she would pull her apron over her head and 'settle down
in God' as she put it. This action didn't block out all the noise but
it was a sign to her children that she was not to be disturbed.

The care of the soul

🐟 *Father, I must find times when I can 'settle down in God'. I
know You will help me find the way. Thank You Father. Amen.*

PLANNED NEGLECT

For reading & meditation – Ephesians 5:1–17
Be very careful, then, how you live ... making the
most of every opportunity ... (vv 15–16)

Another important spiritual exercise is that of *stewardship*. All great theologians of the past have seen stewardship in terms of three things: time, treasure and talents. No soul is fit and healthy unless it is being exercised in the proper deployment of all three.

Take the first – *time*.

Malcolm Muggeridge, the famous broadcaster and wit, said: 'One has to learn what does not contribute – and throw it away.' I thank God for my waste-basket. It relieves me of things that would be a serious waste of my time. People often ask me: 'How have you been able to do all the things you do?' I usually answer: 'By planned neglect.' Certain marginal matters (not family duties and responsibilities) have to be deliberately neglected in order to focus on the task in hand. Sometimes the good has to be sacrificed on the altar of the best.

The care of the soul

JANUARY 26

✎ *O Father, help me say 'No' to lesser things in order to be free to say 'Yes' to the greater things. In Jesus' Name. Amen.*

THE TEST OF TIME

FOR READING & MEDITATION – PSALM 90:1–17

Teach us to number our days aright,
that we may gain a heart of wisdom. (v 12)

Our lives are often ruled by the urgent because we have never taken the time to put things in their proper order of priority. The man who influenced the world most – our Lord Jesus Christ – was never hurried, never flurried and never worried. But He always had time for the things that mattered.

Time past is time over which we have no control; time to come is time concerning which we must search ourselves. The use of time subjects us to a test, trying us as silver refined in a furnace.

A little boy late for school prayed, 'Lord, help me be there on time.' He ran out of his house but stumbled and fell. 'Lord,' he said, 'I asked You to help me, not push me.' Don't let life push you; you will stumble if you do. Discipline your time.

The care of the soul

O God, give me the same disciplined, poised life that Jesus had. Help me manage my time so that I have time for the things that matter. Amen.

GOD OWNS – WE OWE

'The earth is the Lord's, and everything in it.' (v 26)

When I first became a believer I used to resent people taking up a collection every time I went to church. I had only just begun to earn a wage and I hated the thought of giving up part of it. Once I asked my pastor: 'Can't we be followers of Christ without having to give Him access to our money?' I will never forget his reply: 'You can't be a follower of Christ unless He has access to everything you have, including your money.'

The first thing we must do is to establish in our minds the fact that God is the owner of everything; we are owers. This means we are managers, or stewards, of what God has given us. The house or apartment you live in is God's property. The car you drive, the clothes you wear, the food you eat – all belong to God. Viewing life in this way can change your entire perspective.

JANUARY 28 | *The care of the soul*

O God my Father, give me a Biblical mindset on this issue I pray. In Christ's Name. Amen.

STEPS TO STEWARDSHIP

FOR READING & MEDITATION – MARK 11:1–11

'If anyone asks you, "Why are you doing this?"
tell him, "The Lord needs it ..."' (v 3)

First, settle the issue once and for all: you own nothing. Everything you have is a trust. You must give an account of everything you possess to God. Manage your material possessions as *He* likes. Second, acknowledge his ownership by giving one tenth of all you earn. Tithing should not be seen as a maximum but as a minimum.

Third, limit your spending to needs, not luxuries disguised as needs. If you eat beyond your needs you overload the system. It is the same with money and material things. If you have more than you need, give to those who are less fortunate than you.

Fourth, make your will under God's guidance. You have a responsibility to leave something to your family, but consider leaving something as an investment to be used for the kingdom's purposes.

O Father, help me to open the doors of my heart to others. You have entrusted me with things; I want to be worthy of that trust and use them wisely for You. Amen.

SAVED TO SERVE

'But I am among you as one who serves.' (v 27)

We consider now the stewardship of our talents. I am using the word *talents* here generically, that is, to cover all our God-given abilities, whether they are seen as natural or supernatural.

The point is this: whatever your abilities, *they are given for the purpose of serving others*. Every Christian is a servant of God and, as the term suggests, servants *work*. Paul describes his service to God in Colossians 1:29: 'To this end I labour, struggling with all his [God's] energy, which so powerfully works in me.' God supplies us with the power needed to work for Him.

Donald G Bloesch says: 'The spiritual disciplines are to be seen as service in the world.' We are saved to serve – and if we are not serving then quite simply we are not in training to be godly. God asks for our time, our treasure and our talents to be put to his use.

 Lord Jesus Christ, being a Christian demands my all. But then You gave your all for me. Help me never to forget that. Amen.

YOU'VE GOTTA SERVE

FOR READING & MEDITATION – JOHN 13:1–17

...he poured water into a basin and began
to wash his disciples' feet ... (v 5)

Whatever our talents, they have been given to us not simply
for us to enjoy them but so we can serve others. It must be
seen as a discipline. If it is not regarded as a discipline then we will
serve occasionally or do only those things which please or satisfy
us. If the latter then service becomes self-service.

Serving others, it must be said, is not an option for Christians.
Every one of us is expected to serve. Can you imagine an angel
refusing to serve? It is almost unthinkable. Christians who sit on
the sidelines watching others serve and excusing themselves on
the grounds that they do not have enough time, show by their
very actions that they have little idea of what true godliness is.
Remember the old song, 'You've gotta serve somebody'? You have.
You either serve or sag.

*Gracious Father, help me never to forget that my soul is in
training for godliness. Help me to be at my very best for You. In
Jesus' Name. Amen.*

INFLOW/OUTFLOW

FOR READING & MEDITATION – MARK 5:1–20

Jesus ... said, 'Go home to your family and tell them
how much the Lord has done for you ...' (v 19)

Some disciplines relate to inflow; this one is concerned with
outflow. There can be no outflow without an inflow, and the
inflow will come to a complete halt if there is no outflow. To describe sharing as a discipline may sound strange to some, but if
we do not discipline ourselves to do so we may never do so at all.
We should discipline ourselves to share by deed and word what
we have found as we have prayed and read the Word.

Many fail to do this. They are earnest and regular in the way
they take in, but not one person has ever said they are as obedient
in sharing with others as they should be. Time and time again I
have heard older Christians comment, 'If I could relive my life I
think I would be more faithful in sharing my faith with others.'

✎ *O God, forgive me that I miss so many opportunities to share
my faith. Help me discipline myself in this regard. In Jesus' Name.
Amen.*

READY AND ALERT

For reading & meditation – 1 Peter 3:8–22

Always be prepared to give an answer to everyone

... for the hope that you have ... (v 15)

Fear of failure is one of the chief reasons why people fail to share their faith. When we fear something we avoid it. Unless we have a disciplined approach to sharing our faith with others it simply will not get done.

In my youth I was encouraged to make it a discipline to share Christ with someone every day. At the age of eighteen I was drafted into the mines to do a two-year period of National Service. One morning, deep underground, I turned to the young man next to me and asked him if he had ever thought seriously about where he would spend eternity. He said he hadn't, and that led to an interesting few minutes at the end of which he accepted Christ. An hour later this young man lay dead – killed by a large stone that fell from the roof. Were it not for disciplined sharing I might have missed the opportunity to prepare him for eternity.

O God, help us be more disciplined in this direction. Amen.

WITNESS FOR THE DEFENCE

FOR READING & MEDITATION – ACTS 1:1–11

'... and you will be my witnesses in Jerusalem, and in
all Judea and Samaria, and to the ends of the earth.' (v 8)

Our text tells us that Christ's followers are his witnesses.
What does being a witness involve? One preacher described
it like this: 'It means that Jesus is on trial again before the world,
and every one of his disciples is called on as a defence witness.

Suppose we refuse to say a word on his behalf. Then by our
silence we join the prosecution for He said: "He who is not with
me is against me." Or suppose when called we talk about ourselves and our achievements instead of talking about Him. Or
suppose we mumble and apologise and contradict ourselves. We
let Him down – and badly.'

We cut ourselves off from his cross if we do not take up ours,
we cancel the power of his cross for ourselves unless we pass on
its power to others.

The care of the soul

FEBRUARY 3

O God, over the radio and television I constantly hear the
voice materialism persuasively promoting temporal things. Help
me to witness more clearly to You, the Eternal Reality. Amen.

RECEPTIVITY AND RESPONSE

FOR READING & MEDITATION – HEBREWS 6:1–12

Land that drinks in the rain ... and that produces a crop
... receives the blessing of God ... (v 7)

Two matters constitute the heartbeats of the gospel: intake and outflow, receptivity and response. And if both processes are not in operation the Christian heart ceases to beat.

I heard about a husband and wife planning what they described as an 'amicable divorce'. Their nine-year-old daughter had become a Christian, and as they all met to discuss the details the little girl bowed her head and prayed, 'Dear God, You have made such a change in me since I came to know You. Help my mother and father to change also.'

The father and mother looked at each other and as the tears came into their eyes they bowed their heads and received Christ into their lives. The impulse in that little girl's heart to share Jesus is in every one of his followers. It's sad that so often we stifle it.

O God, who could look into your face and not want to share? Inherently I am an evangelist. Help me not to choke the impulse. Amen.

SAY SO

Let the redeemed of the LORD say this – those he
redeemed from the hand of the foe ... (v 2)

Because we have tasted of the Lord we must share our good
news. Psychology advocates a similar form of behaviour; it
says, 'You must be the sharing, communicative type to be healthy.'
If we keep things to ourselves we become self-focused and thus
unhealthy.

One woman found it very difficult to share anything about her
faith with others until she received this suggestion: 'Ask those you
know well about their problems so that you can bring them to the
Lord in prayer.' She put this advice into practice and the results
were astonishing. People were so moved by her expression of concern they opened up to her. She led five of her friends to Christ in
the first month. Yet the secret was not so much the actual method
but the passion which motivated her.

*O God, You have given me the greatest work in the world
– that of bringing others to You. Help me to be faithful and discipline myself to carry it out. In Jesus' Name. Amen.*

IN SIMPLICITY SUBLIME

FOR READING & MEDITATION – MATTHEW 8:14–27

Jesus replied, 'Foxes have holes ... but the Son of Man
has nowhere to lay his head.' (v 20)

The next spiritual exercise is the discipline of adopting simplicity. Let me explain what I mean. Just after my conversion one
of the first tasks assigned to me by my pastor was to study the life
of Jesus as portrayed in the four Gospels. The thing that came
home to me time and time again was the astonishing simplicity of
his lifestyle. The poet Tennyson when writing about a close friend
said: 'He was rich in common sense; in simplicity sublime.' Surely
no one has ever demonstrated the sublimity of simplicity as did
Jesus. His way of life was simple and uncomplicated, in contrast to
that of the Pharisees who were bound by regulations.

If we are to train ourselves to be godly then imitating Jesus in
this respect must be one of our spiritual exercises too. We must
discipline ourselves to be like Jesus and be 'rich in common sense;
in simplicity sublime'.

☞ Simple but sublime Saviour, rid me of all complexity and
artifice. For your own dear Name's sake. Amen.

IT'S ALL TOO SIMPLE

'... unless you change and become like little children,
you will never enter the kingdom of heaven.' (v 3)

Many Christians are being drawn towards a simpler, less complicated lifestyle. Can it be that in a sophisticated age such as this the Spirit of God is prodding his people to show the world that life can be lived to the full and still be simple?

One great difference between the Christian faith and every other religion is its simplicity. To find God, says Scripture (our text), you have to move away from all that is complicated to what is simple. And what can be more simple than a child opening up its hand to receive a gift?

Some people stumble over this very simplicity and reject the Christian message. A man I tried to lead to Christ, a doctor of philosophy, said, 'It's all too simple.' How sad.

O God my Father, I am attracted to the idea of a simpler, less complicated lifestyle. Help me strip myself of all those things that make my life so complex, and move towards a simpler lifestyle. In Jesus' Name. Amen.

OUCH, STOP SQUEEZING!

FOR READING & MEDITATION – ROMANS 12:1–8

Do not conform any longer to the pattern of this world,
but be transformed by the renewing of your mind ... (v 2)

JB Phillips has one of the best translations. It reads: 'Don't let the world around you squeeze you into its own mould, but let God re-mould your minds from within.' What sort of shape is contemporary culture in at the moment? Advertisers make us feel ashamed if we do not wear the latest fashions, drive the most up-to-date car, or eat at the priciest restaurants.

'Society is psychotic,' is the pronouncement of a commentator on worldly affairs. Covetousness is termed ambition, hoarding is regarded as prudent, and greed is defined as being industrious.

Until we understand the thinking of our sick society we will not be able to see how we are being squeezed into the world's mould – how much of the spirit of mammon we have absorbed.

Father, I must ask myself: Am I allowing the world to squeeze me into its own mould? Help me face this question and do whatever is necessary to resist the spirit of the world. In Christ's Name. Amen.

STEPS TO SIMPLICITY

For reading & meditation – Matthew 6:25–33
'But seek first his kingdom and his righteousness, and
all these things will be given to you as well.' (v 33)

'The majority of Christians,' says a contemporary writer, 'have
never seriously wrestled with the problem of simplicity, con-
veniently ignoring Jesus' many words on the subject.' A challenging statement, but is he right? You must answer for yourself.
However, in my opinion he hits the nail on the head. To discipline
ourselves to live more simply is perhaps one of the most demanding of all the spiritual exercises. Simplicity begins on the inside
and works itself out.

(1) *Seek first the interests of the kingdom.* Seek to discipline
yourself to adopt a simpler lifestyle.

(2) *Examine your life.* Are you a person with mixed motives?
Purify your motives inside and your conduct too will be right.

(3) *Resist all attempts to persuade you to buy things for their
status.* Beware of feelings that override your common sense.

O God, I am grateful that You awaken me to the reality of my
situation but so often I am unwilling to do anything about it. Help
me I pray. In Jesus' Name. Amen.

DE-ACCUMULATE

But I have stilled and quietened my soul;
like a weaned child with its mother ... (v 2)

We spend one more day reflecting on some suggestions to help us train ourselves to become godly in relation to the discipline of simplicity.

(4) *Be alert to the possibility of becoming addicted to things.* If there are things you find are not necessities give them up. You must be a slave only to Christ.

(5) *Cultivate a way of thinking that says, 'What can I give away?'* Look in your wardrobe. Can you see anything there in good condition which you rarely use? Give it to someone who is in need. The big word in simplicity, says Richard Foster, is 'De-accumulate'.

(6) *Refuse to be taken in by slick advertising.* And adopt a healthy scepticism to the phrase 'Buy now – pay later'.

(7) *Cut out all affectation in speech and act.* Decide to be fundamentally simple and you will be fundamentally sound. Sublime.

ༀ *Gracious Father, I pray again: Speak the word and release me from the terrible bondage to things. I would be like Jesus – uncomplicated. Help me my Father. Amen.*

FALLACIES ABOUT FASTING

FOR READING & MEDITATION – MATTHEW 6:16–24

'When you fast, do not look sombre as the hypocrites do ...' (v 16)

We come now to consider a discipline which has fallen into disrepute in modern times – the discipline of fasting. Why should something given such a high priority in Scripture be regarded with suspicion by so many Christians today?

One reason is a fear of becoming legalistic. The Church has suffered greatly from legalism in the past. But to say that fasting can draw us back to legalism is to misunderstand Scripture.

Fasting is also viewed with suspicion because our consumer society encourages us to satisfy every appetite every day of our lives. A further reason is that the subject is not proclaimed from modern-day pulpits.

Fasting was taught and practised by our Lord and has been part of the life of the Church throughout its history. The discipline of fasting does wonders for the soul. Put it to the test and see.

 Lord Jesus Christ, You never ask me to do something You did not do Yourself. I confess this challenge I do not find easy. Help me consider and practise it. In Jesus' Name. Amen.

A CUTTING QUESTION

FOR READING & MEDITATION – MATTHEW 9:9–17

'How can the guests of the bridegroom
mourn while he is with them?' (v 15)

Our Lord is being entertained in the home of Matthew the tax collector and enjoying a meal with him and some of his friends. A group of Pharisees question his disciples: 'Why does your teacher eat with tax collectors and "sinners"?'

The disciples of John had given themselves to promoting John's teaching and advocating fasting. They knew too that part of John's ministry was to point men and women to Jesus; how could they do that when He seemed to be more interested in feasting than in fasting? Thus they thrust this question at Jesus: 'How is it that we and the Pharisees fast, but your disciples do not fast?'

Jesus responds by pointing out that it would not be appropriate while the Bridegroom is present for them to fast. Our Lord was giving here an intimation of his death. Well, the Bridegroom *has* been taken away. But how many of his disciples fast?

☞ *Father, I see I need to be more deeply committed. Teach me more, dear Lord. And help me. In Jesus' Name. Amen.*

FEBRUARY 12 | *The care of the soul*

A FUTILE FAST

FOR READING & MEDITATION – ACTS 13:1–12
While they were worshipping the Lord
and fasting, the Holy Spirit said ... (v 2)

The first time I fasted was a few months after my conversion to
Christ. I had overheard several older Christians talking about
fasting, saying that it was commanded in the Bible and should be
practised from time to time by every Christian.

I decided to enter into a three-day fast to see what it was like. It
was one of the hardest, most miserable experiences of my life. All
that happened was that I got hungrier and hungrier, and after
thirty-six hours I broke my fast. Later I realised where I had gone
wrong. I was fasting for the sake of fasting, not for the Lord's sake.
I had no God-given purpose in fasting.

My abstinence was not so much fasting as an experiment in not
eating. And without the intention of discovering God in a greater
way fasting can be a miserable experience. So, although fasting is
an important spiritual exercise, the motivation is crucial.

🐦 *Father, fasting is clearly included in your Word. But I am
still struggling. Help me, dear Father. In Jesus' Name. Amen.*

THE PURPOSE OF FASTING

FOR READING & MEDITATION – EZRA 8:15–23

There ... I proclaimed a fast, so that we might humble ourselves
before our God and ask him for a safe journey ... (v 21)

Many reasons for fasting are given in Scripture. One is to add
power to our prayer lives. Ezra followed this pattern. 'We
fasted and petitioned our God about this, and *he answered our
prayer*' (v 23).

A second reason is to discover God's guidance. This principle is
found in Judges chapter 20. However, fasting does not guarantee
that guidance will be given but it makes us more receptive to the
One who guides.

A third reason is to deepen the expression of an act of repentance. The Old Testament is replete with instances of fasting accompanying repentance. Joel 2:12 is just one verse that records
God urging his people to show their sincerity by fasting. One way
to make sure that repentance is heartfelt is to reinforce the prayer
of repentance with a short period of fasting. Many lives have been
transformed in this way.

 Lord Jesus, You keep bringing me back to reality. Now help
me walk in it. In Jesus' Name. Amen.

A DAY FOR DECISIONS

FOR READING & MEDITATION – HEBREWS 3:1–15

' Today, if you hear his voice,
do not harden your hearts ...' (v 15)

Biblical fasting must always have a spiritual purpose. There can be little doubt that God rewards fasting undertaken for a spiritual reason with great blessing.

My writings on fasting may have made some people feel guilty, and that they might therefore decide to fast simply to rid themselves of those feelings of guilt. Examine your heart on this issue. I would like to feel that you are drawn to fasting for the right reasons, not the wrong ones. Think the matter through carefully. Fasting is commanded by God and is clearly taught in Scripture. That does not mean you must start today. Pray and ask God to guide you. All you need to say is, 'Lord, I recognise this truth and I am willing to follow your leading.' God will guide you as to the right times, the appropriate times. Focus on the other spiritual exercises and the Lord will count your willingness to fast as the deed done.

🐾 *My Father, I see this is a day for decision. I yield to You. In Jesus' Name. Amen.*

GOOD FOR THE SOUL

For reading & meditation – Psalm 32:1–11

Then I acknowledged my sin to you
and did not cover up my iniquity ... (v 5)

The next spiritual exercise we examine is that of confession and forgiveness. Confession is owning up to God and others about the wrongs we have done, and forgiveness is being willing to wipe the slate clean regarding any who have wronged us.

Take *confession*. An old saying goes like this: 'Confession is good for the soul.' It is. On this point modern psychology agrees with the teaching of Jesus. CH Barbour says: 'When the conscience condemns the ego for wrong actions it may rid itself of the depressing sensation by means of spiritual catharsis [cleansing] through confession.'

To find oneself in the wrong and do nothing about it is to condemn the self to live with a self one cannot respect. Repression is just as bad. When we drive guilt into the subconscious and shut the door on it we do not get rid of it. There it festers and sets up an irritation.

Lord Jesus Christ, help me to rid my soul of all corrosive guilt through the exercise of confession. In Jesus' Name. Amen.

TO WHOM DO WE CONFESS?

FOR READING & MEDITATION – PSALM 51:1–19

Cleanse me with hyssop, and I shall be clean;

wash me, and I shall be whiter than snow. (v 7)

If we are to get rid of guilt we must admit our fault, expose it to the light of Christ and resolve it by confession.

All wrongs must be confessed to God. Access to God has been made easy through Jesus. Our Lord's awful purity made sinners feel condemned, yet his purity was not forbidding but forgiving. If you dare to expose your heart to his heart you will find not merely relief but release. And you must find that, for with guilt in your system your soul will turn sour. Then if we have wronged others we must make confession to them too. Confession must be always as wide as the circle of offence.

One final point: confession must be wholehearted, without anything held back.

🐦 *Lord Jesus Christ, I wince and yet I know that what You say is true. Help me to confess all sin and have done with it. I don't just want to be better, I want to be whole. In Jesus' Name. Amen.*

I CAN'T FORGIVE

FOR READING & MEDITATION – MATTHEW 6:1–15

'But if you do not forgive men their sins,
your Father will not forgive your sins.' (v 15)

What should we do when others have wronged us? We should forgive. But you protest: 'I can't forgive.' Then I say very quietly, very tenderly, but also very solemnly: if you won't forgive you can never be forgiven. By refusing others forgiveness you are breaking down the bridge over which you yourself must pass, namely that of forgiveness.

But perhaps you are still defensive and saying to yourself, 'I can forgive but I can't forget.' Well take those words and apply them to the Lord's Prayer. How glad we should be that God does not forgive in that way. He removes the record of our sin from his book of remembrance.

Oh, the wonder of God's forgiveness When we see how much we have been forgiven that in itself should be enough to send us out filled with joy to forgive others.

O God, perhaps I haven't really seen how much I have been forgiven. I open myself to a new understanding of that today. In Jesus' Name. Amen.

WHAT'S EATING YOU?

FOR READING & MEDITATION – COLOSSIANS 3:1–17

... forgive whatever grievances you may have against one another.
Forgive as the Lord forgave you. (v 13)

At one time I had to consult a doctor over this matter of indigestion. He asked, 'What sort of frame of mind are you in when you eat?' Astonished I said, 'What has that got to do with it?' He replied, 'It's got everything to do with it. It's not so much what you eat but what's eating you. If you aren't in a good state of mind you had better lay off eating until you are.'

He was right. I realised my indigestion was caused by a harboured resentment. I forgave the person I was resentful towards and my digestive tract gave me no further trouble. The stomach was made for goodwill, not illwill. Goodwill sets it up and illwill upsets it!

The same is true of the soul. Flush all bitterness out of your soul as you would flush a toxic substance out of your body.

O God, Help me to constantly practise forgiveness. For how can I be forgiven if I do not forgive? In Jesus' Name. Amen.

THE WAY OF THE MASTER

For reading & meditation – Ephesians 4:17–32

Be kind and compassionate ... forgiving each other,
just as in Christ God forgave you. (v 32)

During World War II, when Japan was determined to wipe out
Christianity, a test was devised. A cross was laid on the ground
and when one suspected of being a Christian was brought before
the tribunal he or she was told to walk upon the cross. Those who
refused were killed and those who did were freed.

I saw one of those crosses in South Korea. It had on it a faint
reproduction of the face of Christ, almost worn away by the many
who had stepped on it. Would it be going too far to suggest that
when we refuse to forgive we trample on the cross? When we
refuse to forgive we bring pain to the heart of our Lord.

What greater joy can there be than having a soul free of guilt?
Confession and forgiveness are the way to achieve that. But both
must be full and frank and free.

*Lord Jesus Christ, my Saviour and my God, help me to forgive
those who have wronged me. Amen.*

KEEP ON KEEPING ON

For reading & meditation – Hebrews 12:1–17

... let us run with perseverance
the race marked out for us. (v 1)

M y one-time pastor used to end every service by pronouncing the benediction, then adding these words, 'Keep on keeping on.' I can think of no better definition of the word than that.

So often our lives are strewn with the wreckage of good beginnings which became poor endings. A recording of the London marathon race frequently focused on a man who looked as if he wouldn't make the first mile. But he kept on and on, and although he reached the finishing point long after the winners, he did at least *finish*. A large number dropped out but he carried on doggedly. The crowd at the finishing line gave him as much applause as they did the winner.

As the song goes: 'It's not how you start but how you finish.'

🐦 *Father, help me to keep on keeping on. However many of these exercises of the soul I have begun, help me to keep on with them. I don't want to begin well but finish badly. I want to start and end well. In Jesus' Name. Amen.*

THE HELPER

FOR READING & MEDITATION – DEUTERONOMY 5:22–33

So be careful to do what the LORD
your God has commanded you ... (v 32)

Physical training experts tell us that exercise must be regular if
it is to do the body any good. It is the same with the soul.

Some might say, 'But I'm the spontaneous type who finds it difficult to develop disciplined habits.' If you are a Christian then the
Holy Spirit dwells within you to make you like Christ. You may not
be a disciplined or persistent person, but the Holy Spirit is.

Listen to this: 'He who began a good work in you will carry it
on to completion until the day of Christ Jesus' (Phil 1:6). The Holy
Spirit's task is to produce within you the desire and power to train
yourself to be godly. Your task is to co-operate with the Spirit. As
you yield yourself to Him your natural temperament will come
under his control. He will help you persevere.

*Father, thank You for the help You provide for me through the
Holy Spirit. Strengthen my will so that I become even more willing.
In Jesus' Name I pray. Amen.*

The care of the soul

FEBRUARY 22

LAST BUT NOT LEAST

For reading & meditation – Galatians 5:16–26

But the fruit of the Spirit is love, joy, peace ...
gentleness and self-control. (vv 22–23)

People often comment, 'You must be a very disciplined person.'
Actually my temperament is by nature more spontaneous than
disciplined. One of my school reports even criticised me for being
'lacking in self-discipline'. The Holy Spirit turned me into a disciplined person. All the credit goes to Him and to Him alone.

Self-control is a fruit of the Spirit. It comes last on Paul's list,
though that does not mean it is least in importance. I make the
point because many systems, ancient and modern, would put self-
control first.

The Christian message is that the Holy Spirit's direction produces a self-controlled person. But note: we do not gain the Holy
Spirit through self-control; we gain self-control through the Holy
Spirit. We begin with love – love for Christ and love for others –
and end up with self-control.

*Father, some have so much self-control that they appear rigid,
tense and nervous. I want the self-control that stems from the Holy
Spirit's control – the kind that is supernaturally natural. In Jesus'
Name. Amen.*

TOGETHER

FOR READING & MEDITATION – 1 THESSALONIANS 5:12–28

The one who calls you is faithful ... (v 24)

When Christians express self-control by practising spiritual disciplines they find themselves growing in godliness. Timothy Jones discovered the Holy Spirit's role in helping him develop a disciplined prayer life. Let him tell you himself.

'I was drawn into the presence of One who had the power to keep me close. I found my focus shifting from rigour to grace, from rigidity to relationship. I soon realised that this was happening regularly. I was praying much more. I became less worried about the mechanics and methods and was more motivated. And God so cares for us that I realised anew ... He Himself helps us pray. I can't explain how it is that the Holy Spirit prompts us and produces in us the desire to persevere in things. All I know is – He does.'

God is faithful in keeping us. Our task is simply to yield ourselves to Him.

We will make it – together.

Father, thank You that perseverance does not involve just my effort or just your effort. It is the combination of the two. I am eternally grateful. Amen.

THE CHRISTIAN STRUGGLE

For reading & meditation – 1 Timothy 4:1–16

For physical training is of some value,
but godliness has value for all things ... (v 8)

Have you ever heard anyone say, 'I thought the Christian life would be a bed of roses. I never realised it would be such a struggle'? Over the years I have heard this, or a similar statement, hundreds of times. Such thinking results from wrong teaching – teaching that raises false hopes in people.

Storms and high seas are as much the lot of Christians as they are of non-Christians. Giving our hearts to Christ means that He is with us in life's storms, not that storms will never buffet us. All Christians struggle from time to time – but we have the help of God in those struggles.

Progress in Christian growth is made through a combination of God's effort and our effort. This is important New Testament teaching. Those who teach 'Let go and let God' are giving only half the truth. The other half is 'we labour and strive'.

Father, I know that the struggle is not my struggle but our struggle. This makes all the difference. Thank You my Father. Amen.

PRACTICE MAKES PERFECT

For reading & meditation – Proverbs 12:1–15
Whoever loves discipline loves knowledge ... (v 1)

The path that leads to godliness is the practice of spiritual disciplines.

John Guest, an American writer, included in a magazine article the story of a farmer who went to collect eggs from his chicken shed. However, on his way he noticed that the yard pump was leaking so he stopped to fix it. After that he saw that a pitchfork needed a new handle. When he had finished fitting the new handle he noticed something else needed doing ... It was late morning by the time he finally got to collect the eggs. Does the farmer's morning remind you of your own spiritual life? Is it sporadic and spontaneous rather than directed?

I have often been told, 'You play the piano beautifully.' Accomplished pianists, however, realise when they hear me play that my playing is the result of spontaneity rather than disciplined practice. Some people's spiritual lives are like that. They impress others with their spontaneity but deep down they lack discipline.

Heavenly Father, I pray that You will help me undergird my spontaneity by sound self-discipline. In Jesus' Name. Amen.

IN TRAINING FOR ETERNITY

For reading & meditation – Ephesians 3:1–13

... according to his eternal purpose which he
accomplished in Christ Jesus our Lord. (v 11)

'The future of the world,' said Dr E Stanley Jones, 'is in the
hands of disciplined people.' What did he mean? In another
part of his writings he added: 'The future of the world is in the
hands of people who are disciplined to the highest ends.' Modern
life is compartmentalised, specialised and it lacks *total* meaning.

Just as the spokes of a wheel hang loose without a hub so do
the powers of life unless they are fastened to the central hub – the
Lord Jesus Christ. He and He alone gives total meaning to life. This
is why we must keep God and eternity in view while practising
spiritual disciplines.

Imagine the difference it would make if we saw everything from
the viewpoint of God and eternity. To view discipline as simply relating to time is short-sighted. We are in training for eternity.

*Father, what a thrill it is to know that the blessings that come
from spiritual gymnastics extend beyond time into eternity. In
Jesus' Name I pray. Amen.*

GREAT GAIN

FOR READING & MEDITATION – 1 TIMOTHY 6:1–10

But godliness with contentment is great gain. (v 6)

Over the past few weeks we have looked at ten of what theologians call 'the classic disciplines' : (1) regular reading of the Scriptures, (2) prayer, (3) worship, (4) seeking solitude, (5) stewardship, (6) sharing the faith, (7) simplicity, (8) fasting, (9) confession and forgiveness and (10) perseverance. They are, to borrow a phrase, 'the Himalayas of the spirit'. Miss out on one of these and the soul will not remain healthy and fit.

Development of the soul does not just happen. The soul has to be trained to be godly. The way to God is through Christ, and the way to godliness is through the spiritual disciplines. Are you willing to commit yourself to ongoing training for godliness?

Let me give the last word to Vance Havner, a blunt and direct country preacher from the United States: 'The alternative to discipline is disaster.'

O God, nothing repels me more than the thought that I might experience spiritual disaster. By your grace I will give myself to training my soul for godliness. My resistance is gone. Now onward for ever. Amen.

THE WAY OF SIMPLICITY

FOR READING & MEDITATION – 2 CORINTHIANS 11:1–15

I am afraid … your minds may … be led astray from
your sincere and pure devotion to Christ. (v 3)

No one has had a more brilliant intellect than Paul, yet he saw
the danger of depending on intellect rather than on Christ.
He points out that Eve was led away because she put her own
reasoning before God's reasoning. The instructions she and Adam
had been given were simple, uncomplicated, and easy to understand, but she allowed the serpent to muddle her thinking. And
when sinful action followed sinful thinking, the whole universe
was catapulted into what we now describe as 'the Fall'.

The faith to which we are called by Christ is the simplest thing in
all the world – simple without being simplistic. When we take that
which is so simple and complicate it by our additions or subtrac-
tions, we make it more difficult for ourselves and others to follow.

*O God, forgive us that we have taken that which You designed
to be so simple and straightforward and turned it into something
so tortuous and complicated. Amen.*

MARCH 1 | Simplicity in Christ

IN SIMPLICITY SUBLIME

FOR READING & MEDITATION – MATTHEW 22:23–40

… an expert in the law, tested him … 'Teacher, which is
the greatest commandment in the Law?' (vv 35–36)

I wonder if the lawyer who stood up to ask Jesus the question that
is before us today realised that our Lord's answer was a stroke
of genius. Jesus reduced all the laws and commandments to just
two: love to God and love to man. If, as someone has said, 'Beauty
is an absence of superfluities', then there must have been none
more beautiful than the Lord Jesus Christ – certainly in character
and perhaps even in appearance. No one has ever demonstrated
the 'sublimity of simplicity' more than He. His entrance into this
world was simple. He was born not amidst pomp and finery, but
in a humble cattle shed. He spent his early years not as a king or
a military commander but as a carpenter.

His words were simple and straightforward, the language of
simple men. In Him there was no pretence, no useless verbiage.

🕊 *O simple but sublime Saviour, cleanse me so that I might be
as You were when on earth. Amen.*

WHOLE FACTS

For reading & meditation – Matthew 5:27–37

And do not swear by your head, for you
cannot make even one hair white or black. (v 36)

I want to explore with you how to communicate with others.

Our Lord's words were whole facts. The religious men of Christ's day tried to make their language impressive and give their statements an added sharpness by swearing on everything they could think of. Jesus told them: 'Do not swear at all: either by heaven, for it is God's throne; or by the earth, for it is his footstool ... Simply let your "Yes" be "Yes", and your "No", "No" ...' (vv 35, 37).

He was saying – you don't have to strengthen the truth by an oath, trying to get this, that, and the other. You ought to so live that an oath is unnecessary. We never see Christ trying reinforce his remarks with an oath. His words were always true. This must be our system of communication also.

O God, help me that my 'Yes' always means 'Yes' and my 'No' always means 'No'. Father, this is how your Son lived. Help me, dear Lord. In Jesus' Name. Amen.

WHOLE TRUTH

FOR READING & MEDITATION – MATTHEW 5:33–48

'... let your "Yes" be "Yes", and your "No", "No";
anything beyond this comes from the evil one.' (v 37)

I want to focus on the words that form part of our text : '... anything beyond this comes from the evil one'. What Jesus is saying here is that the kingdom of God is built on truth and goodness; the kingdom of darkness is built on evil and a lie.

The devil is behind all lies, and in one place our Lord said of him: 'When he lies, he speaks his native language, for he is a liar and the father of lies' (John 8:44).

Evil is always tangled, roundabout, subversive, and complex. Goodness is always a reduction of life to simplicity. Just analyse a lie, for example. Lies are always roundabout, complicated, and deceiving. Truth is straightforward, uncomplicated, and open. Jesus spoke the truth, all the time. And following close to Him, so will we.

☞ *O Yes, Father, I must stay close to your Son. Help me not to make this a matter of self-effort but of simple depencency on Christ. In his strong and powerful Name I ask it. Amen.*

THE WORST THING ...

FOR READING & MEDITATION – LUKE 20:20–26

'Teacher, we know that you ... teach the way
of God in accordance with the truth.' (v 21)

The whole thrust and energy of the universe which God designed and created is simple, uncomplicated, and built on truth.
There are great mysteries, of course, but no lies. Scientific laws are
upheld by truth.

Gravity, for example, will not lie; it is as true in one country as
it is in another, as reliable in Jerusalem as it is in Japan. It has
often been pointed out that the word *evil* is the word *live* spelt
backwards. Satan delights to take what God does and try to reverse it – to move life in the opposite way to that in which it was
designed to go.

People who tell lies become extremely anxious. This anxiety is
picked up by a machine known as a 'lie detector'. We are built for
truth, and any departure from it can be picked up on the outside.

*Father, a lie demeans me, but the truth develops me. May I be
a person of truth. In Jesus' Name I pray. Amen.*

WHAT NEED FOR CRUTCHES?

FOR READING & MEDITATION – EPHESIANS 4:17–32

Do not let any unwholesome talk come out of your mouths ... (v 29)

Our Lord had no need to bolster what He said with oaths, for everything He said was according to the truth.

Several ministers have shared with me their concern at the increasing use of profanities and swear-words among Christians. When Christ came into my life one of the first things He did was to clean up my language. I have always been intrigued as to why people swear and I once made a special study of this issue. This is what I found: those who curse and use swear-words are unsure of themselves so they try to make their statements more emphatic by profane assertion.

Swearing is not the sign of strength, but of weakness. The more you swear, the weaker your statements. Swearing and profanity are the crutches people use when they feel unsteady and insecure.

O God, forgive me if my words and language do not reflect my confidence and trust in You. Please do what is necessary to bring me to the place of dependent trust. In Jesus' Name. Amen.

THAT OTHER 'WORD'

FOR READING & MEDITATION – MARK 2:1–12

... and he preached the word to them. (v 2)

We are told that when Jesus entered into a house in Capernaum, people hearing He was in the home crowded into the room to listen to what He had to say. 'He preached the word to them.' What does Mark mean: 'He preached the word to them'? What was that 'word'?

I think that what Mark is telling us here is that it was the 'word' amid the multiplicity of words.

When people heard our Lord's words they recognised that there was something that could only be explained as the 'word' in the midst of words. Everyone has heard of the famous oration given by Abraham Lincoln. A great orator spoke prior to Lincoln, and although his words were powerful, in the multiplicity of words there was no 'word'. When Abraham Lincoln spoke, people heard in his words the 'word' of democracy.

How wonderful it would be if others would hear in our words the 'word' of truth.

Yes, dear Father, help me bring the 'Word made flesh' to men and women. In Jesus' Name I ask it. Amen.

SPEECH THAT IS SIMPLE

For reading & meditation – Matthew 26:57–66; 27:11–14

'… Tell us if you are Christ, the Son of God.' (26:63)

The more we put our Lord's words and language under the spiritual microscope, the more we see how He demonstrated the art of reducing speech to simplicity. I heard a politician once say of another in Parliament, 'Words were given to us to communicate our meaning, but the member opposite seems to have found another use for them.' Such an accusation could never be laid at Jesus.

He refused to answer the high priest's pointless question, yet when He was asked directly whether or not He was the Son of God, his reply was clear as crystal: 'Yes, it is as you say' (26:64). Later, when accused by the chief priests and elders, He made no reply. When a relevant issue arose He was simple and direct. When an irrelevant issue arose He maintained a majestic silence.

Often we get so bogged down in dealing with the irrelevant. We need to catch the simplicity and directness of our Master.

O God, I long to be like my Master in thought, word, and deed. Amen.

CLEANSED SPEECH!

FOR READING & MEDITATION – COLOSSIANS 4:1–15
Let your conversation be always full of grace,
seasoned with salt ... (v 6)

How ought we as his modern-day disciples to live?

We ought to go over the way in which we communicate and relate to others and decide to bring our speech and our language in line with our Lord's. Therefore, we must surrender our speech to God for cleansing. For some it may mean cutting out all affectation, all unreality, all insincerity, all weasel words, all talking for effect, all complicated and convoluted statements. As Christians, everything about us ought to ring true, especially our speech. We must avoid all loose statements about people, refuse to stick labels on them, and make sure that our words are a revelation, not of fantasy, but of fact.

The Chinese say, 'Words are the sounds of the heart.' Let's make it our aim to ensure that our heart and our words have the same sound – the sound of simplicity and love. When we are fundamentally simple, we are fundamentally sound.

My Father and my God, make me like a weaned child, weaned from all that complicates. Amen.

VOCABULARY ADJUSTMENT

FOR READING & MEDITATION – TITUS 2:1–15

'In your teaching show ... soundness of speech
that cannot be condemned ...' (vv 7–8)

I have put down my New Testament many times when reading
the sayings of Jesus and sat back enthralled at the way He put
words together. CS Lewis is a modern-day example of such a word-
smith. He once said he would no more use ornate language than
ornate clothing.

In one of the churches I pastored, whenever I stood up to preach,
a young man in the congregation would take a book out of his
pocket and begin to read. When I asked him why he did that he
said, 'You're not being real man. You are using words to impress,
not teach.' I was devastated – devastated but disciplined.

If we, as Christ's modern-day disciples, speak in such a way to
the men and women of this age that they hear only words, then
can we blame them if they too take out a book and read it?

*Father, I surrender my vocabulary to You for pruning. Cleanse
me of all unreality and remove all veneer. In Jesus' Name. Amen.*

SIMPLE – BUT NOT EASY

'… unless you change and become like little children,
you will never enter the kingdom of heaven.' (v 3)

Our Lord reduced speech to simplicity. Now we look at the way He reduced the big issue of how we enter the kingdom of God to utter simplicity of spirit.

Saying entrance into the kingdom of God has been made simple is not the same as saying it is easy. Why, the very simplicity puts some people off. A university professor who heard me speak on the text, scoffed at much of what I said. He told a friend of mine after the meeting, 'The ideas the speaker presented were not demanding enough. He made the way into the kingdom of God too easy.' He missed the point entirely. I had not claimed it was easy – just simple. And it was not me who said that anyone who will not receive the kingdom of God like a little child will not enter into it, but Jesus.

O God, teach me in my relationship to You to become less complicated and more like a little child. In Jesus' Name I pray. Amen.

BEING IN CONTROL

FOR READING & MEDITATION – ROMANS 10:5-21

'... if you confess with your mouth, "Jesus is Lord," and
believe in your heart ... you will be saved.' (v 9)

Becoming childlike is one of the most difficult things for us to
do. Adults who have been knocked about a bit by the world
are more cautious, more judicious, more wary.

One of the things that used to surprise me in the early days of
my ministry was to hear highly intelligent and well educated people say as they were being led to Christ, 'Is it really that simple?'
They expected to be faced with some complicated theory, or required to memorise a creed.

We would much prefer to do something to save ourselves than
to adopt a trusting childlike attitude, because strenuous self-effort
gives us a feeling of being in control. The one thing above all others which our human nature abhors is the feeling of not being in
control. For some it is easier to struggle than to trust. Easier, but
not productive.

Simplicity in Christ

MARCH 12

O Father, teach me how to curb this strong desire to be in control and lead me to a more childlike trust. Amen.

GOD HAS NO GRANDCHILDREN

FOR READING & MEDITATION – JOHN 1:1–14

… born not of natural descent, nor of human decision
or a husband's will, but born of God. (v 13)

Our text tells us that we can't expect to get into God's kingdom because our parents were Christians, because we were
born in a Christian country or born in a Christian home. As someone put it, 'God has no grandchildren.'

The second thing is that entrance comes not by the whipping
up the will, but by surrender of the will.

Third, the only way is by simplicity of spirit: 'Yet to all who received him ... he gave the right to become children of God' (v 12)
it all hinges on the receiving. You don't find God through climbing
a ladder of self-effort, to find Him on the top-most rung. You find
Him at the bottom of the ladder where He came down to us through
his Incarnation.

MARCH 13 | Simplicity in Christ

O Father, as I listen to the gospel story once again, it all seems
so amazingly simple. Help me not to complicate it by my egocentric
tantrums. I surrender to You now. Save me. In Jesus' Name. Amen.

HERE FOR THE TAKING!

FOR READING & MEDITATION – DEUTERONOMY 30:11–20

… the word is very near you; it is in
your mouth and in your heart … (v 14)

No other religion has a God who came down to earth to die for
those who want to know Him.

Other religions claim that we have to strive to find God. Christianity says the very opposite – you simply have to let God find
you. In other words, stay where you are, don't struggle, and simply call out to God that you want Him to save you. As has often
been said, 'Religions are man's search for God; Christianity is God's
search for man.' That is why there are many religions, but only
one gospel.

The kingdom of God is as close as your next breath. If you reach
out to try and earn it, you reach too far. It is here. And it is here
for the taking!

*O Father, You bring all this so close, I cannot but find You,
for You are really finding me. Help me see that salvation comes
not through egotistic striving but through simple receiving. I come
Lord. I come. Amen.*

TO LIVE LIKE MR MURRAY

FOR READING & MEDITATION – GALATIANS 1:11–24

... to reveal his Son in me ... (v 16)

We who are Christians must watch that we do not complicate what Christ has made simple.

I heard of a pompous bishop in India who asked some confirmation candidates, 'What does it mean to be a Christian?' He expected an involved and complicated theological answer, so imagine his surprise when one of the group said, 'To live like Mr Murray.' Mr Murray was the missionary who had taught them. Their definition of Christianity might be thought by some to be too simple. But was it? I think not. They had caught the heart of Christianity – to reflect the nature and character of Jesus.

There are many theological knots I have not yet untied. But the basics are simple. It is a matter of trusting a Person. And unless you give your trust to Christ, you will never be able to get into the kingdom of God. The Christian life begins with simplicity of spirit.

Gracious and loving heavenly Father, help us see that great issues are always simple. In Jesus' Name. Amen.

THE FATHER'S STYLE

FOR READING & MEDITATION – MATTHEW 11:20–30

'... you have hidden these things from the wise and learned,
and revealed them to little children.' (v 25)

Our Lord wants simplicity to be characteristic of his followers also.

The Amplified Bible puts our text in these words: 'You have hidden these things from the wise and clever and learned, and revealed them to babes – to the childish, the untaught and unskilled. Yes, Father, such was your gracious will and good pleasure.' It is the chosen purpose of God to reveal things to the simple-hearted because He delights to do so. As CS Lewis put it: 'It is the Father's style.'

A great educationalist stated, 'The first step in education is the admission of how much you do not know.' It might upset those who like to feel they are always in control, but the fact is this – in the kingdom of God the simple-hearted see and know; the rest are blind.

O Father, help me to admit how much I do not know so that I can become an eager candidate in the school of the Spirit. In Jesus' Name I pray. Amen.

TWO KINGDOMS – ONE LAW

FOR READING & MEDITATION – MATTHEW 5:1–12

'Blessed are the poor in spirit, for theirs is the kingdom of heaven.'

Of course an effort has to be made to study and research, but the true unfolding comes only through surrender. To learn we must first listen.

I agree with my scientist friend's comment that surrender of heart and mind is as true in the realm of nature as it is in the realm of grace. When I meet a scientist I usually ask him (or her) this question, 'Are the discoveries of science mainly the result of an aggressive spirit or a humble spirit?' Nine times out of ten the answer is, 'A humble spirit.'

The scientist who has no humility will discover the secrets of the universe, but not half as much as the one who sits quietly before the universe in an attitude of surrender. It is the same in the kingdom of grace.

Father, thank You for showing me this truth, that just as the kingdom of nature yields its most precious secrets to those who are humble-minded, so it is also in the kingdom of grace. In Jesus' Name. Amen.

AN OPEN SECRET

FOR READING & MEDITATION – MATTHEW 13:1–17

'The knowledge of the secrets of the kingdom of heaven
has been given to you, but not to them.' (v 11)

Moffatt's translation of our text reads: 'It is granted you to understand the open secrets of the Realm of heaven.' God has built into his universe both in the realm of nature and of grace some wonderful and precious secrets, but they are uncovered more by humility of mind than an aggressive search. Much more depends on the attitude rather than the workings of the mind. Electricity was in the universe from the time of creation, but not until Benjamin Franklin conducted his experiments was its potential discovered. The possibility of being heard around the world was there from the beginning, but it was Marconi who was the first to detect it.

'The secret of discovering things,' says Dr Stanley Jones, 'is a spirit – a spirit of self-surrendered humility.' The first step is to be humble, to be teachable, to cease struggling, stop fighting – and listen. Someone is speaking – and speaking authoritatively.

Gracious and loving Father, sharpen my mind, my brain power, but even more – sharpen my attitudes. In Jesus' Name. Amen.

HEART-FIRST INTO LIFE

FOR READING & MEDITATION – MATTHEW 21:1–11

'... See, your king comes to you,
gentle and riding on a donkey ...' (v 5)

Jesus reduced the matter of understanding the things that relate to the kingdom of God to humility of mind, not brilliance of mind.

Those who demand of life instead of listening to what life demands of them end up tired, disconsolate, and dispirited. HG Wells declared that the psychologist can stand alongside the preacher and say that unless you are free from all preoccupation with self-interest there is a disintegration of the personality.

Jesus said that the path to growth, development, and knowing involves a freedom from arrogance, self-interest, self-centredness. In other words – simple-heartedness. The world tends to applaud those who go into life head-first – with the right kind of intellect. God applauds those who go into life heart-first – with the right kind of attitude.

Father, I see that whilst You are not against intellect – indeed You designed it – You long above everything that I might have the right attitude of my heart – the attitude of Jesus which I see in the text for today. Amen.

A POP-UP OF SURPRISES

... the things that come from the Spirit of God

... are spiritually discerned. (v 14)

An acquaintance of mine, a PhD in theology, told me that he was not really a Christian. He came into the ministry, pastored a church for several years, but did not know Christ in a personal way. One night an evangelist preached at his church, and the minister realised that he did not know Christ in the way the evangelist was presenting Him. So he left the pulpit, knelt at the front, and took Christ as his personal Saviour. Immediately the Bible became 'a pop-up of surprises'.

Our text makes clear that we can never grasp the Bible's secrets by intellect alone. The secret is not a trained mind, but a simple and humble spirit. I'm glad Christ reduced this matter to such a simple level. It puts the divine secrets within the reach of us all.

Father, I am thankful that though You do not deride the intellect, You do not depend upon it as being the vehicle for your revelation. Blessed be your Name for ever. Amen.

Simplicity in Christ

MARCH 20

TWO WAYS TO BE RICH

FOR READING & MEDITATION – LUKE 12:13–21

'… a man's life does not consist in
the abundance of his possessions.' (v 15)

We focus on Jesus' words that life is to be found in being rich towards God.

I love the story of the missionary who welcomed a newcomer to the mission station, 'Make a list of all the things you think you need and I will show you how to get along without them.' Jesus is saying that life is not to be found in possessions.

A bishop of the Early Church, who was a remarkable example of the virtue of contentment, was asked his secret. 'It consists in nothing more that the right use of my eyes. I first look up to heaven and remember my principal business is to get there. Then I look down to the earth and call to mind how small a place I shall occupy when I die and am buried. This enables me to keep a right perspective.' I say his philosophy was simplicity sublime.

Gracious and loving heavenly Father, help me want more of You and less of things. In Jesus' Name. Amen.

40 ACRES FOR FREE!

FOR READING & MEDITATION – PHILIPPIANS 4:10–20

I have learned the secret of being content
in any and every situation … (v 12)

We live in a world that is terribly preoccupied with things. Survey after survey shows that people equate happiness and contentment with their physical circumstances. They say, 'If you have a nice home, a happy marriage, an adequate income, a wide circle of friends, congenial work and good health, you can be happy.' But life does not confirm this view. True contentment is found in the right inner attitude, not in material possessions.

An old Quaker advertised 40 acres of rich farm land to anyone who could prove that he was perfectly satisfied with what he had. Far too many for him to interview individually gathered outside his house. So the Quaker said, 'All thou who art perfectly satisfied with what thou hast, raise thy hands.' Everybody raised their hands. 'Then why dost thou want this land?' asked the Quaker. The crowd looked at each other in silence and one by one they shuffled away.

🖙 *Lord Jesus Christ, give me the mind that was in You. For your own dear Name's sake. Amen.*

STEWARDS, NOT PROPRIETORS

<small>FOR READING & MEDITATION – PROVERBS 19:20–29</small>

The fear of the LORD leads to life: Then one
rests content, untouched by trouble. (v 23)

God is not against us possessing things, but He is against them possessing us. It may be right for some Christians to give up their material possessions. For example, CT Studd, the famous missionary, gave away his inheritance to become a servant of Christ on foreign fields. But God does not require that of everybody. Other Christians may find God endowing them with material possessions because He wants them to be stewards of those things and use the resources for the advancement of his kingdom.

The 'simplicity that is in Christ', as it relates to possessions, is first and foremost a philosophy, a mindset. It is a mindset that says that though I be stripped of certain things, it will in no way affect the peace that resides within my heart. When you can live independently of things then you are rich indeed.

<small>*Lord, how complicated life can become when there are many possessions. Help me to see that whatever I have has come from You. In Jesus' Name I ask it. Amen.*</small>

<small>*Simplicity in Christ*</small>

<small>MARCH 23</small>

DISCONTENT!

FOR READING & MEDITATION – MATTHEW 5:21–30

'And if your right hand causes you to sin,
cut it off and throw it away.' (v 30)

How simple life would be if we would only follow the words of our Master and see that life consists not in the abundance of our possessions but the richness of our relationship with God. The more our hearts become entwined around material things, the more unhappy we shall be. Hence the extremely strong words in the passage before us today – words that should be meditated upon and taken to heart.

A cartoon depicted two fields divided by a fence. In each field was a mule, and each mule had its head through the fence, eating grass from the other mule's pasture. The cartoon depicted also that the mules, in their effort to eat the grass in the other's pasture, had got caught up in the fencing and were unable to extricate themselves. One word at the bottom of the cartoon summed it all up – 'Discontent'.

Simplicity in Christ

Father, *help me grasp the fact that I am rich in proportion to the number of things I can afford to let alone. In Jesus' Name. Amen.*

GIVING WAY TO THE SIMPLE

FOR READING & MEDITATION – 1 TIMOTHY 6:3–16

But godliness with contentment is great gain. (v 6)

I have talked to many people whose businesses have crashed, but I remember one in particular, a fine, spiritually-minded man who responded to my question as to how he was handling his new circumstances in this way, 'I think little about what I haven't and a lot about what I have.' 'Considering what you have gone through,' I asked him, 'how would you now define Christianity?' He thought for a moment and said, 'The complicated giving way to the simple.' I was amazed at his insight and came away conscious more of being helped than of having been a helper.

May I suggest that you go over your life and see if there are any mixed motives? But remember – all self-examination ought to be done in God's presence and after a prayer inviting Him to search your heart. Then look at what God uncovers. If it is clear there are complicated motives then surrender them into the hands of God.

🌱 *O God, far too often I am a nervous, anxious and complicated person. Make me simple and unafraid. Amen.*

THE WAY – FOR EVERYTHING

'I am the way and the truth and the life.' (v 6)

Christ reduced life's most troublesome and perplexing personal problems to the realm of simplicity. When I say 'personal problems' I am thinking of those things which drive people into counselling – difficulties in relating, temper losses, inner turmoil, depression, obsessive or compulsive thoughts, high anxiety, fear of failure, and so on.

I have trained in theology and psychology, pastored six churches, and have over forty years' experience as a counsellor. In all that time I have noticed when dealing with people's personal problems that although they were so complex that it sometimes took months to understand and comprehend them, the actual solution, the key that unlocked the difficulty, was always simple.

'All great personal problems,' said a Harvard University professor, 'are a reduction from complexity to simplicity.' How I wish he would have added – the simplicity of Jesus.

My father and my God, I have found the way not to live; now let me find the way to live – and live abundantly. So hold me close. In Jesus' Name I ask it. Amen.

Simplicity in Christ

HOW PROBLEMS ARISE

FOR READING & MEDITATION – JOHN 10:1–10
'I have come that they may have life, and have it to the full.' (v 10)

People's problems can be extremely complex, sometimes needing many hours to unravel.

Consider first how problems arise in the personality. As a result of Adam and Eve's original sin in the Garden of Eden we live in a fallen world where our bodies do not function in the way in which they were designed. And this physical malfunction can have a direct influence on our moods, our attitudes, and our outlook on life. This is why my advice to people who are struggling with serious emotional problems is to first have a medical check-up to ensure that the problem is not coming from a physiological malfunction.

Spiritual problems (and I include in that phrase what people call 'psychological' problems) are also a consequence of living in a fallen world. When problems arise that sometimes get beyond our control, the key that unlocks the difficulty, is always simple: a close and rich relationship with God.

Simplicity in Christ

O Father, entering into the fullness is something I can't always do. Help me in the Saviour's peerless and precious Name. Amen.

TRUST AND OBEY

FOR READING & MEDITATION – 1 PETER 2:1–12

... the one who trusts in him will never be put to shame. (v 6)

Time and time again I have seen depressions lift when people grasped the reality of God's purpose for their lives and entered into it with abandonment and joy. And what about anxiety neurosis? When such people learn to take his promises more seriously, something more powerful takes place. Two lines of an old hymn put it most effectively:

Trust and obey, for there's no other way
To be happy in Jesus, but to trust and obey.

Can it really be as simple as the old hymn suggests? The answer is 'Yes'. However, to take that simple truth and pass it on to someone in the same way that a doctor gives out a prescription, without taking the time (sometimes a long time) to build a bridge of empathy and understanding, is to violate the nature and the Spirit of our Lord and Saviour Jesus Christ.

O God, save me from the insensitivity that barges into the lives of those who are in the midst of deep personal problems and says 'Just trust Jesus'. Amen.

PSYCHOLOGY – OR CHRIST?

FOR READING & MEDITATION – JEREMIAH 6:9–16
Stand at the crossroads and look; ask for the ancient paths ... (v 16)

Christian counselling is now at a crossroads in many countries of the world, as more and more turn to psychological theories that leave out Christ. Many (thank God not all) are settling for solutions that substitute fascinating ideas for reality, and interesting humanistic theories for the tried and tested truths of Scripture. I am not against people studying the subject of psychology, but that is not what is going to help people when they are caught up in the throes of inner conflict. Something is wrong when we in the Church turn from the simplicity that is in Christ to theories that have no compatibility with Scripture.

If the Christian Church does not take a stand against the humanistic ideas concerning people-helping that appear to be flooding into it, then I tremble for the Church of tomorrow.

🙏 O God my Father, forgive us as your people that we so often go cap in hand to the world for ideas. Help us to put the emphasis on Jesus. In his Name I pray. Amen.

A GROWTH-STOPPER

FOR READING & MEDITATION – JUDGES 2:16–23

They refused to give up their evil practices and stubborn ways. (v 19)

What has amazed me as a veteran Christian is how I can maintain a fairly good relationship with God on the surface yet still depend deep down on my own resources for holding my life together. I know the answers to my problems, whether they be personal or otherwise, are to be found in Jesus – that is a simple and established Biblical fact. But when you ask me to trust the invisible God to make my life work, rather than depending on the things I can see and I know have worked for me over the years, I am conscious that within me is a stubborn commitment to independence that is sometimes quite frightening.

Independence, I suspect, is the real problem that hinders our development as persons and the giving of ourselves in abandoned trust to Christ.

O Father, break all stubbornness within me – the stubbornness that blames You for not coming to my aid when really it is me not being willing to come to You. Forgive me, my Father. In Jesus' Name. Amen.

ONE RESPONSIBILITY

FOR READING & MEDITATION – JOHN 15:1–17

If you remain in me ... ask whatever you wish,
and it will be given you. (v 7)

What are the implications of following our Lord in simplicity?
You are weaned from the necessity of wanting things because you have the source of all things – Christ Himself. Your world of entertainment becomes simple, you draw from within. You 'draw waters from your own well' as Proverbs 5:15 puts it.

You are weaned also from the necessity of success. You don't have to succeed. You simply sow the seeds of love, truth, and then watch them bring forth fruit of their own accord.

From now on, say to yourself every day: I have one overall responsibility – to live in union with God. That reduces life to the simple and the vital. Focus on that one thing and all else follows. So simple, yet so sublime.

My father and my God, life has been so complex and complicated and now, at long last, I am coming to the simple. I accept my primary responsibility – to be in union with You. I am a child again, simple, happy, unafraid. Amen.

NON-DEFENSIVE LIVING

FOR READING & MEDITATION – LUKE 12:1–12

When you are brought before ... authorities, do not worry
... for the Holy Spirit will teach you ... (vv 11–12)

Another area of life which our Lord simplified so beautifully is
that which relates to our personal identity. If we are not sure
of ourselves and have no inner security we tend to become defensive in an attempt to prove to others that we are secure.

Some Christians think the above words of Jesus teach us that if
we are involved in a court action we ought not to defend ourselves.
Indeed, one has to combat lies and dishonesty with the truth.

The thought underlying the words of Jesus in our text has more
to do with what today we call 'defensiveness': the attitude we develop when we are unsure of ourselves and, due to the anxiety this
causes deep within, we relate to others from a position of weakness rather than strength. But why be complicated when you can
be simple? Life is so much better the Jesus way.

Simplicity in Christ

*O living Christ, give me your security, your steadfastness. For
your own Name's sake. Amen.*

APRIL 1

THAT'S TRUST!

For reading & meditation – Psalm 62:1–12

My soul finds rest in God alone;

my salvation comes from him. (v 1)

Those who live in a constant state of defensiveness because they are not really sure of themselves and of their resources end up living complicated lives. They go around nervously trying to explain things.

Secure persons will, when called to explain their behaviour, do so in a clear, gentle, and loving way. But if the explanation is not accepted, they will feel no inner need to remonstrate with an accuser and press their point.

A Christian I know, a leader of a church, was accused of something of which he was innocent. He explained the facts, but his explanation was not accepted and he was removed from the pulpit. I wondered why he hadn't done more to protest his innocence. With assurance he said, 'Truth is on my side ... the months will speak against the hours.' Within six months he was vindicated and went back to the pulpit. Now that's trust.

O God, help me to know the experience of the psalmist: 'My soul finds rest in God alone.' In Jesus' Name I pray. Amen.

DEFENSIVE PROJECTION

FOR READING & MEDITATION – I SAMUEL 19:1–10

'My father Saul is looking for a chance to kill you.
Be on your guard …' (v 2)

Defensive people are always anxious people. And to cope with the anxiety they become more and more defensive. Thus life becomes more and more complicated. Defensiveness can ruin relationships and paralyse potential.

Defensiveness is described in modern-day language as projection. This takes place when we attribute to someone else our own thoughts and feelings. We can't face these things in ourselves so we project them on to others and condemn them from a safe distance. Christians who react with deep anger and condemnation when they discover faults in others may well be exhibiting this type of defensiveness.

When you read the story of King Saul in the book of Samuel you certainly get a picture of a man who, although he was called to be king, felt deeply inadequate for the task. His trust was largely in himself and not in God – a poor foundation on which to build a kingdom.

O Father, show me how to put my trust in You. In Jesus' Name I pray. Amen.

SECRET SINS

Then Nathan said to David, 'You are the man!' (v 7)

Even God-fearing people can act defensively – and not know that they are doing it. David was so self-deceived in relation to his sin with Bathsheba and later the murder of Uriah that his judgement became distorted. When Nathan came and presented to him his barbed little parable, David overreacted and wanted the man in the story put to death. Because David had not dealt with the issues which had been going on in his own life, and had not repented of what without doubt are the grossest of sins – adultery and murder – he unconsciously projected his inner self-conflict on to someone else.

The writer Elizabeth Connors said: 'What we repress in ourselves we project on to others and try to get rid of our guilt feelings by transferring them onto others.' Such an attitude is not worthy of a committed Christian, and we must pray as David in Psalm 139: 'Search me, O God, and know my heart ...' (v 23).

Simplicity in Christ

APRIL 4

O God, cleanse me from every secret sin. This I ask in Christ's dear Name. Amen.

THE WORD THAT IS ALIVE!

FOR READING & MEDITATION – HEBREWS 4:1–13

For the word of God ... penetrates even to dividing
soul and spirit, joints and marrow ... (v 12)

Another symptom of defensiveness is denial. Denial, when present in our hearts, blocks the road to being an open and non-defensive personality.

Denial is the refusal to admit to whatever is true. It is a denial of reality. The opposite of denial is integrity, or, if you prefer – non-defensiveness. The work of keeping reality at bay drains our energy that ought to be directed into positive and productive living.

The kind of denial I am talking about is an unconscious one and arises from those parts of us where the truth of God has not quite penetrated. That is why we must take to heart the truth of the scripture before us and allow the Word to evangelise not just a part, but the whole of our personalities.

🖝 Lord, evangelise my heart. Let the Word that is alive penetrate to the deep springs of my being so that even my unconscious is invaded by You. In Jesus' Name I ask it. Amen.

ONE WORTH FOLLOWING

For reading & meditation – John 7:37–52
'No-one ever spoke the way this man does ...' (v 46)

Defensive living is not an option when it comes to following in the footsteps of the Master. Comb the record of Jesus' life in the Gospels and you will not find one occasion when He was defensive. He spoke clearly about life's issues and chose the right words to convey his thoughts. But He would never be drawn into protracted arguments, and, having made his point, He never pressed it to the stage where He became tendentious. He was simple, unaffected and unafraid.

How different are our lives when compared to his – and how much more complicated!

The defensive live more by fear than faith. The non-defensive are not afraid to confess to mistakes because, being essentially right (but not arrogantly so), they are never afraid to be sometimes wrong. How much more simple life is when we are free from defensiveness.

Lord Jesus Christ, my Master, teach me how to walk in your footsteps and be a less defensive person. Show me how to make a start this very hour. For your own dear Name's sake. Amen.

THE DIVINE PERSPECTIVE

For reading & meditation – 1 Corinthians 1:18–31

'Let him who boasts boast in the Lord.' (v 31)

Yet another area of our life which our Lord simplified for us is that which has to do with the concept of success. We live in a time which has been labelled as 'The Success-Oriented Age'.

Now let me say right away that I see nothing wrong in working to be successful, or in setting clear goals. I think the saying 'People don't plan to fail but fail because they don't plan' has some merit. But for a Christian there is much more to it than that.

The most successful man who ever lived, our Lord Jesus Christ, failed by all the human standards that are used to measure success. He possessed no property, left no money and when He was taken by wicked men and crucified, most of his followers deserted Him. All He left were some simple seeds sown in hearts which, watered by the Spirit, have spread throughout the earth and transformed the centuries.

My Father and my God, give me, I pray, a universal view – your view of things. In Jesus' Name I pray. Amen.

GOD ALONE GIVES SUCCESS

FOR READING & MEDITATION – 1 CHRONICLES 22:1–13

Then you will have success if you are careful to observe
the decrees and laws that the LORD gave ... (v 13)

I am not condemning the drive to succeed or the need to establish
clear goals and move forward to successful ends. I am seeking
to raise a caution against getting into bondage to success. Many
people, if they succeed, feel complete as persons; if they fail, they
feel destroyed.

You do not have to succeed in everything you do. All you have
to do is be true to what you believe God is leading you into. Act
from this simple premise: pray about everything, do what is right,
and leave the results to God. Then the results will always be right.
It is impossible that the right thing should have the wrong result
in the long run.

You do not have to despise success, you simply must not depend on it. When God and his presence in your heart is the priority then you can have it or do without it.

O God, help me not to be in bondage to success. In Jesus' Name. Amen.

GOD-GIVEN SUCCESS

FOR READING & MEDITATION – 2 CHRONICLES 26:1–23

As long as [Uzziah] sought the LORD, God gave him success. (v 5)

King Uzziah experienced the best type of success – God-given success. However, once he became powerful, pride set in and led to his downfall. He thought he could take over from the priests and offer incense on the altar. When the priests confronted him he turned on them with fierce rage, whereupon God struck him with leprosy which remained upon him until the day he died.

It is possible to build our life with God and then to allow that success to go to our heads. No one is free from this possibility. We are never more close to failure than during the period of our greatest success if we fail to recognise God's hand in our achievements.

When we discover that we can do many things well, a consuming pride can invade us. Never cease to give thanks to God for all your accomplishments. After all, without Him you could do nothing.

O Father, forgive me if I have become self-dependent and carried away with my personal skills and accomplishments. In Jesus' Name. Amen.

APRIL 9 | *Simplicity in Christ*

A FORMULA FOR SUCCESS

And the peace of God … will guard your hearts
and your minds in Christ Jesus. (v 7)

It is imperative that we as Christians do not allow ourselves to be
brainwashed by the world – a world, by the way, on which Satan
has a strong and powerful grip. There is nothing wrong with ambition, providing we be weaned from the notion of the necessity of
success before we achieve success, so that when it comes we know
how to handle it.

I urge you to give as much attention to the means as you do to
the end – prayer, meditation on the Scriptures, and dependency
on the Holy Spirit.

Rejoice in God more than in what you accomplish. Never be
anxious, because God is in final control. Pray about everything
and never cease to be thankful. And let God's peace be the sentinel
that stands on duty at the door of your heart.

*Loving heavenly Father, burn these precious words from
Scripture into my heart so that they will become a guiding force
in my life. Make me weaned from all that complicates. In Jesus'
Name. Amen.*

HOW TO HANDLE FAILURE

For reading & meditation – Romans 8:28–39

And we know that in all things God works
for the good of those who love him ... (v 28)

I know some will be more concerned with how to handle failure.
If failure is part of your life at this moment then the following
will help you.

First, be willing to accept the loss with a genuine willingness to
experience the pain. It's by mourning a loss that you recover from
it. Second, consider how you may have contributed to the failure.
Decide that you will learn from the situation. Where an apology is
necessary, be ready to give it. And where forgiveness is needed, be
prepared to offer it.

Third, surrender the whole situation into God's hands. When you
are a Christian and you are fully committed to God, then you have
Him to help you turn the setbacks into springboards. And admit it
– you can learn more from failure than you can from success.

*O God, make me alert to listen to Wisdom, Goodness, and Re-
demption. I long to be God-guided. Teach me the art of learning
what You want me to learn. In Jesus' Name. Amen.*

WASHING FEET

FOR READING AND MEDITATION – JOHN 13:1–17

... he poured water into a basin and
began to wash his disciples' feet ... (v 5)

I have one more thing to say about the issue of success – learn to measure it by heavenly standards and not earthly ones. Dr Paul Rees, an American preacher, said: 'If you want a picture of success as heaven measures it, of greatness as God views it, don't look for the blaring of the bands on Broadway; listen rather for the tinkling of water splashing into a basin while God incarnate, in a humility that makes angels hold their breath, sponges the grime from the feet of his undeserving disciples.'

Failure must always be viewed from the divine perspective. As Woodrow Wilson once put it, in words that have now become famous: 'I would rather fail in the cause that someday will triumph, than triumph in a cause that someday will fail.' That sums up the message of Christianity as well as anything I know.

Lord Jesus, what the world sees as failure You see as something different. Give me your insight, your wisdom, your gaze at everything. Amen.

THE WAY TO SERVE

For reading & meditation – John 17:1–19

'I have brought you glory on earth by
completing the work you gave me to do.' (v 4)

An area of life that seems to create complications for many
Christians is that of commitment. There are so many things
that need to be done, and so little time in which to accomplish
them. How do we discharge our Christian duty and calling without falling into the trap of overcommitment?

Jesus beautifully simplified this area of life. He kept his heart
open only to the things God required of Him. Thus He was able to
achieve more in three and a half years of ministry than many
achieve in a lifetime.

I challenge anyone to find a page in the Gospels where Jesus
appears to be overcommitted. He moved through his ministry at a
leisurely pace. Whatever He did, He did well, and He approached
important issues with great seriousness. But He was never pres-
sured. He modelled for us all the way in which we are to serve.

🖛 *Father, show me what You want me to do. And I have all the
time in the world for that. Amen.*

WE ARE DRIVEN!

FOR READING & MEDITATION – MARK 6:30–44

'Come with me by yourselves to
a quiet place and get some rest.' (v 31)

It is certainly true that Jesus was a zealous worker. But there is never any suggestion in the Gospels that He became emotionally exhausted. Never once do we see Him caught up in a frenzy of activity. The passage before us shows Jesus deliberately seeking relief from the fast pace of ministering to others, and He advises his disciples to do the same.

Our Lord's life was one of beautiful and simple balance. He accomplished everything the Father sent Him to do – everything – and He accomplished it without ignoring those essential times of rest and relaxation.

I do notice warning signs in the Church that more and more believers are tending to see their identity in terms of their performance and their work. Unless we are careful, we will finish up being people who not only work at worship, but who worship work.

Simplicity in Christ

APRIL 14

☞ *Lord Jesus, help me to know your will for me, and to respond to the will of others only when it is your will. In Jesus' Name I pray. Amen.*

BALANCE – PERSONIFIED!

For reading & meditation – Luke 5:12–16

But Jesus often withdrew to lonely places and prayed. (v 16)

Workaholics, churchaholics, overcommitted believers – slow down. Those who were brought up indoctrinated with a strong work ethic struggle with this because we have been programmed to believe that the more we do the more God loves us.

I look back and wonder how I allowed myself to get caught up in responding to requests for ministry that did not carry the Lord's signature. How I wish someone had forced me to look in detail at the life of Christ from the perspective I am talking about now. I looked only at the things He did and avoided looking at those occasions when He did nothing.

It is important not to get the impression from what I am saying that Jesus strolled nonchalantly through his ministry. He was never aimless, half-hearted, or discursive. But neither did He come anywhere near getting an ulcer either. He was balance personified.

Beautiful and balanced Son of God, give me such a sense of security that I will work because I am saved, not in order to be saved. Amen.

MIMICKING GOD

FOR READING & MEDITATION – EPHESIANS 5:1–21

Be imitators of God, therefore, as dearly loved children … (v 1)

What a strange command: 'Be imitators of God.' It's even stranger still when you realise the word 'imitators' comes from the Greek word *mimeomai* from which we get the English word *mimic*. We are being told that as believers we ought to mimic God.

There are many ways, of course, in which we can imitate or mimic God, but the particular one I want to look at now is developing a proper balance between activity and leisure. The very first being we read about in the Bible who took a rest is God. He created – then rested.

Why did God rest on that seventh day? He did it in order to set us an example. The Almighty knew full well that our creative times must be followed by restful times. That is the way God has ordained things. If we are to be imitators or mimics of God then we must see to it that we too make rest a priority.

APRIL 16 | *Simplicity in Christ*

O Father, help me to honour You by imitating You. In Jesus' Name. Amen.

BE STILL

FOR READING & MEDITATION – PSALM 46:1–11

'Be still, and know that I am God.' (v 10)

Every one of us must come to terms with the value of tranquillity, slowing down, moving apart from the hustle and bustle of life and enriching our lives in quiet and deep communion with God. 'Be still, and know that I am God.'

The statement is designed to show us that when we spend time with God in the stillness, the Almighty has an opportunity to interact with us in ways that deepen our knowledge of Him. Then we are less likely to go off and involve ourselves in activities which are not glorifying to Him.

So just in case you are rushing over these words eager to get into the activities of the day, let me repeat what I have been trying to get across in my notes for today – knowing God requires that at times we be still.

O Lord, what fools we are when we allow ourselves to be slaves chained to schedules of our own making. Show us ways to put our world together in the way You want it to be. In Jesus' Name. Amen.

DEMONSTRATION NEEDED

FOR READING & MEDITATION – MATTHEW 6:25–34

'… do not worry about tomorrow,
for tomorrow will worry about itself.' (v 34)

Nodding in recognition of what I have been saying about over-commitment will do you no good unless you determine to act. It is not inclination that is needed now, but demonstration.

First, decide to spend more time with God in prayer. Ask God to show you what things He wants you involved in and what things you ought to cut out.

Second, your identity as a person is not found in your work. You are who you are because of your relationship to Jesus Christ.

Third, build into your schedule definite times for leisure and relaxation. Make yourself aware of the beautiful sights and sounds of the world which God has wrapped around us. If you decide to do what I suggest, five years from now you will look back and be glad you did.

Loving heavenly Father, may we become people like your Son, committed to You, working for You, yet relaxed and leisurely in our approach to life. Help us enjoy life, not endure it. In Christ's name we pray. Amen.

DEALING WITH TEMPTATION

For reading & meditation – Matthew 4:1–11

Jesus said, '… it is written …' Then the devil left him … (vv 10–11)

The matter of temptation can sometimes cause people great distress and consternation. But the manner in which we ought to deal with temptation has been made clear and simple by the example of our Master.

Christ was presented with three strong and powerful temptations. First, He was tempted to turn stones into bread. But Jesus saw it as a ruse to shift his gaze away from the face of the Father. Second, standing on the highest point of the Temple, He was invited to throw Himself down. Our Lord saw this as an attempt to get Him to prove something He already knew was true. Third, Satan offered Christ a shortcut to the kingdoms of the earth.

Our Lord resorted to the precise words of Scripture. Could anything be more simple?

Simplicity in Christ

☞ *O Master, I am no match for Satan. But when I have your Word, then he is no match for me. Deepen my conviction of this. For your own dear Name's sake. Amen.*

TWO KINDS OF POWER

FOR READING & MEDITATION – PSALM 23:1–6

... he restores my soul. (v 3)

Christ handled the temptations in the wilderness by depending on Scripture. Of all his resources, He chose only to lean on the Scripture given to Him specifically for this occasion. Note the word *specifically*, for this is the key to handling temptation. It is not enough to know a few verses of the Bible. We must soak our minds in Scripture so that we are able to select the right word for the right occasion.

John Sherrill, a prolific writer, claims that in the Bible there are manna verses and arsenal verses. On a manna verse we can regularly feed and draw deep inspiration or encouragement; an arsenal verse we store in our memories to use when encountering some fierce temptation. The well known psalm before us contains both on which we can feed and lean over and over again.

What energy and power lies hidden in the Word of God. To ignore it is to live dangerously.

My Father, help me soak my mind in Scripture so that it becomes my very energy and life. In Jesus' Name I pray. Amen.

DOUBTS MAKE A DIFFERENCE

FOR READING & MEDITATION — GENESIS 3:1–13

... God did say, 'You must not eat fruit from the
tree that is in ... the garden ...' (v 3)

Our Lord demonstrated the principle of rebutting Satan's temptations by drawing his attention to the written Word of God so beautifully and simply in his encounter with Satan in the wilderness.

What would have happened if Eve had used this principle in the Garden of Eden? She did actually draw Satan's attention to it, but moved away from God when she listened to the serpent's suggestion that He might have had a less than loving motive in restricting them in this way.

We must be sure that we have no doubts about the Word of God. The formula for rebutting Satan, is to refer him to the precise words of Scripture, and also believing it to be true ourselves.

Simplicity in Christ

APRIL 21

🐦 *O God, give me I pray an unshakeable confidence in the power and veracity of your Word. Teach me how to doubt my doubts and believe my beliefs. I want a faith that cannot be shaken by Satan. Help me, my Father, Amen.*

'ALL' MEANS 'ALL'

For reading & meditation – 2 Timothy 3:1–16

All Scripture is God-breathed … (v 16)

Although the best method of dealing with Satan's temptations is to draw his attention to the precise words of Scripture, more is needed if the temptation is to be overcome. We must link ourselves to an appropriate passage in absolute trust and believe it to be the infallible Word of God.

One of my concerns about many in today's Church who cast doubts on the authority and veracity of the Scriptures is that in that position they are quite defenceless when it comes to spiritual warfare. Satan has them at his mercy. They may quote the Word of God, but if they don't believe it to be inspired and authoritative then they are an easy prey for the adversary. I urge those reading these lines who, although committed to Christ, do not have a high view of Scripture, to think again. God has told us: 'All Scripture is inspired of God ...' (v 16 RSV). All! Don't pick and choose.

O Father, once again I ask, help me have confidence in the Bible. In Jesus' Name. Amen.

SAY SO!

I don't quite know how it works, but there is power to be experienced in speaking the Word of God out loud. I have witnessed this power in my own life many times, and in the lives of others also. Of course, critics of this idea point out that Jesus wasn't the only one who spoke out the Word of God in the temptation in the wilderness. Satan did too.

Obviously, the difference was that the Word spoken by Satan was the wrong Word for the occasion and used to deceive; the Word uttered by Christ was the right Word for the occasion and spoken to uphold the glory of God. Satan knows how to build an argument, but he has no defence against the Christian who knows the Word, believes the Word, and is committed to the Word. Simple!

Yes Lord, it's simple, but I recognise that my carnal nature likes to have a hand in my defence and longs to come up with something I can take pride in. Deliver me from this. In Jesus' Name. Amen.

APRIL 23 | *Simplicity in Christ*

A MORE EXCELLENT WAY

For reading & meditation – John 5:31–47
'You diligently study the Scriptures because you
think that by them you possess eternal life.' (v 39)

When Jesus was tempted in the wilderness He did not try
clever mental manoeuvres, or repeat trite little sayings.

It appeals to our carnal nature to come up with all kinds of
mental tricks to deal with temptation. These ideas tend to feed our
ego. In my time I have read many intriguing and complicated
formulae for dealing with temptation, and while I am not prepared to say they have no value at all, there can be little doubt that
the best way is to follow the example of our Lord and go right
back to the clear words of Scripture. God's Word is imperishable,
unimpeachable, and infallible.

Unless we spend time with this Book and soak our minds in its
truth, then however clever we are, we are no match for Satan at
the time of temptation.

*Father, I am grateful for the inspiration I find in Christian
writings, but I see I must measure these by the Scriptures. Help me
always to do this. In Christ's Name I pray. Amen.*

APRIL 24 | Simplicity in Christ

LIFE IS FOR LOVING

For reading & meditation – Mark 12:28-34

'... love [God] with all your heart ... and
... love your neighbour as yourself ...' (v 33)

Throughout time philosophers and thinkers have wrestled with
the question of why we are here. In the passage before us now
we see our Lord once again simplifying the whole matter. Life is
loving, says Jesus. We are here to love God, and to love others.
Could anything be more simple?

Love is the atmosphere for which we were made. When we
breathe in love, God's love, and give it out, we are functioning in
the way we were designed. That is why being in a loveless atmosphere makes us feel choked, stifled. Little children who are not
loved develop all kinds of problems – physical, mental, and spiritual. As Dante put it: 'It is love that spins the universe.' I would
add, 'And it is lovelessness that puts the brakes on it.'

Simplicity in Christ

O Father, I see so clearly that when we find love we find everything, for love glorifies all. Help me fulfil my destiny. In Jesus'
Name. Amen.

THE GREAT SIMPLICITY

For reading & meditation – Hebrews 10:19–31

And let us consider how we may spur one another
on towards love and good deeds. (v 24)

We said yesterday that living is loving. Without love we suffer
from a kind of nostalgia which affects our spirits, our souls
and our bodies.

I once heard a medical doctor say that lovelessness hinders digestion and dries up gastric juices. Clearly, the body is made for
love, just like the soul.

I am convinced that to act on love is realism – the only realism.
To act on anything but love is to complicate issues. It introduces a
disruptive tendency which, sooner or later, ties a situation in knots.
Inherently, everything is made to work in love's way, and in no
other way. If we try to make life work in any other way than love
we work our own ruin. Love has been described as 'the Great Simplicity'. By that standard lovelessness is 'The Great Complexity'.

*O God my Father, help us not to be driven to love by necessity,
but to choose it by an act of volition. Help me love as You love,
dear Father. In Jesus' Name. Amen.*

LOVE CAN'T FAIL

For reading & meditation – 1 Corinthians 13:1–13

Love never fails. (v 8)

Listen to the words again: 'Love never fails.' Never.

What Paul is saying in making this statement, is this – when you act on love then, even though you may not gain what you hoped you might gain, you have not failed, for you have put a deposit into the situation which works in ways that are completely unknown to you. For one thing, you yourself are the better for acting on the basis of love. And so are those who are the recipients of your love. They may not feel it at the moment, but something is working in their lives that is positive and good.

The loving person always wins because, not least, he or she becomes the more loving for giving out love. 'Love never fails' – never fails to enrich the giver of love. It just can't fail. And for the same reason, the unloving act can never succeed.

Father, since love is the victory, then I cannot fail if I love. Help me to practise love on everything and everybody I meet. I ask this in Jesus' Name. Amen.

MORE PRECIOUS THAN GOLD

FOR READING & MEDITATION – 1 JOHN 2:1–14

But if anyone obeys his word, God's love
is truly made complete in him. (v 5)

If you should succeed in getting your way by an unloving attitude
or deed, you won't really be succeeding, not in the true sense of
the word, because the unloving attitude or deed registers itself in
you, becomes you. Your very being is demeaned by the unloving
attitude or deed. To put it in modern-day language – the payoff is
in the person.

A woman who was always intent on changing people listened
to a sermon brought by a visiting minister, and saw where she
had been going wrong. She wrote to a friend, 'How right the
preacher was about everyone being an island and needing love.
When one finds Jesus, He does the transforming from the inside
out. We are not capable of changing anyone. But to love them and
help them find Him is the answer.' As she viewed people through
his eyes and his love, they looked different, they were changed
without her trying to change them.

*Lord Jesus, help me not to try to change people – just to love
them. Amen.*

FAITH THAT 'WORKS'

FOR READING & MEDITATION – GALATIANS 5:1–10
The only thing that counts is faith expressing itself through love. (v 6)

Some believe that faith is the energy that drives Christianity. But it is not – what drives Christianity is faith that 'works by love' (KJV).

Many Christians feel their faith needs protection. If they would go out and love, that would be protection for the Christian faith, for it would be a proclamation of the Christian faith. Our faith must work by love because that is the only way it can work. Love is the applied edge of the Christian faith, or, as the Americans put it: the place where the rubber meets the road. I heard a preacher say once, 'Faith is love in shoes. It goes out to serve – the least, the last, and the lost.'

When our faith works by love then it shows we have faith in love. If we go down loving then we go down, but we will not stay down. For love, as we have been saying, never fails. It is love or nothing.

Father, help me to make love my motive, my method, my atmosphere, my goal. Amen.

THE WORLD'S SICKNESS

FOR READING & MEDITATION – 1 JOHN 4:7–21

... if we love one another, God lives in us and
his love is made complete in us. (v 12)

Love is not an elective course in the school of life; it is a necessity. It is a must. Alfred Adler, psychiatrist, put it this way: 'All
the ills of personality can be traced back to the fact that people do
not understand the meaning of the phrase: It is more blessed to
give than to receive.'

So if you approach Christ through the door of science or the
door of Scripture you come out at the same place – love. Only to
the extent that we love do we live.

Show me a church which has love in it and I will show you
people who know how to live. Where there is love, there is the
true Church. And nothing, absolutely nothing, can atone for the
lack of it.

🙏 *Father, I cannot love in my own strength. So I open my heart
to the flow of your love. Live in me, then I know You will also love
in me. In Jesus' Name I ask it. Amen.*

UNSUNK AND UNSINKABLE?

For reading and meditation – 2 Corinthians 4:1–14

... we may be knocked down but we
are never knocked out! (v 9 PHILLIPS)

Can we have such an experience of God within that no matter
what happens outside of us, we can remain reasonably secure and poised? If we can't, then we are sunk. If we can, then we
are not only unsunk, but unsinkable.

It is a fact that modern man and many Christians also, appear
to lack inner serenity and poise. The strained type of living which
we have developed is issuing in shattered nerves, disrupted lives,
broken homes, overflowing hospitals and overworked social services. We seem to know everything about life except how to live it.

Those of us who profess to be followers of Jesus Christ must put
our lifestyle where our mouth is. Then our words will have at-
tractiveness and power. Cultivating that lifestyle must become our
main occupation.

*Gracious and loving Father, help us learn the lessons of how
to be inwardly poised. We want our witness for You not just to be
with our lips, but with our lives also. Teach us to live. In Jesus'
Name. Amen.*

AN IMPOSSIBLY HIGH STANDARD?

FOR READING AND MEDITATION – MATTHEW 5:1–12

Rejoice and be glad ... for in the same way
they persecuted the prophets ... (v 12)

Our text for today shows that we are expected to demonstrate poise in even the most difficult situations.

I am not hard with Christians who are caught up in tragic circumstances, but we are expected to demonstrate poise in even the most difficult situations.

This matter of gaining inner serenity and poise is extremely important, for without it, our witness to the world is just a matter of words. The most powerful form of evangelism is when our lips and lifestyle coincide. What is the use of getting up in our pulpits or on crusade platforms and announcing that Christ can make a dramatic difference in our lives if our own lifestyle does not demonstrate this to be the case?

Would our Lord ask us to do something that is impossible to achieve? In Christ we have a Saviour who can help us reach it.

O Father, help me to realise that the Christian life is not my responsibility, but my response to your ability. Amen.

A NEW DAY WITH GOD

FOR READING AND MEDITATION – ISAIAH 43:14–21

Do not remember the former things …
Behold, I will do a new thing … (vv 18–19 NKJV)

Don't miss what God is saying to you today. If there has been an inability on your part to maintain your spiritual poise in the midst of difficult circumstances, face up to the fact right now, admit it, then give it to God. Do not turn your past failures into a spiritual club and beat yourself with it.

Remember this – we hang on to feelings of failure and guilt because they can provide us with an excuse for not moving forward. God will cancel out the past mistakes and help you start all over again. So let there be no more rationalisations, no more hanging on to the past.

This is a new day – a day for moving on in God. Put all your failures behind you – and reach out for his hand.

The Christian way to serenity and poise

MAY 3

☞ *My Father and my God, I see I must not stay with useless regrets but move on in You. I do so now – contritely and willingly. Amen.*

DEFINING THE TERM

For reading and meditation – John 10:1–16
... I have come that they may have life, and that
they may have it more abundantly. (v 10 NKJV)

Spiritual poise is the ability to function effectively in the midst of
difficult and frustrating circumstances and maintain, or quickly
recover one's balance, when beset by adverse pressures.

To be a person who is spiritually poised does not mean that you
will always be perfectly calm and composed and feel no negative
emotions. That would not be in accordance with reality, for even
Jesus had occasions when it was said of Him that his soul was
'troubled'. Spiritual poise means that no matter what negative
events and circumstances come your way, you have within you a
God-given ability to recover quickly and deal with whatever has
happened with a clear mind and an unresentful spirit.

To live this way is not just living – but living abundantly. And
that is the very thing which Christ promises, not just to some but
to all his followers.

*O Father, help me see that if I am not living abundantly, the
fault is not Yours – but mine. Amen.*

OUR DESIRE – GOD'S INTENTION

FOR READING AND MEDITATION – COLOSSIANS 1:3–18

... all things were created by him and for him. (v 16)

People who spend their lives studying and working with the physical laws of the universe tell us that all the mechanisms of physical life work toward one supreme end – poise and stability. Life on this planet is designed by God with a driving purpose which is the maintenance of balance and poise and if it lacks that, it perishes.

If it is true that all the mechanisms of physical life work toward this end, then should we be surprised to discover that law in the spiritual life as well? Hardly, for the God of the Bible and the God of biology are one. So when we seek to develop spiritual serenity and poise, we are not working against the universe, we are working with it. The Almighty has written this intention and demand into the whole of his creation, the spiritual as well as the physical.

The Christian way to serenity and poise

O God my Father, I am grateful to find that when I desire inner poise, I am in line with your intention. Thank You, dear Father. Amen.

STABILITY DOES NOT JUST HAPPEN

FOR READING AND MEDITATION – HEBREWS 1:1–14

… upholding and maintaining … the universe
by His mighty word of power … (v 3 AMP)

The Christian way to serenity and poise

The thrilling thought that the universe has been designed with a supreme driving purpose – the maintenance of stability and poise – reflects the character of God. God is a being of perfect serenity and poise and if you cannot see that in the texts of the Bible, then all you have to do is study the texture of creation. The God of the Christian religion and the God of life are one and the same God.

The universe is designed by a loving Creator to enable all his living creatures to remain poised and stable, no matter what the circumstances. Would God do this for the physical and not for the spiritual? He could not and still remain God.

My Father and my God, when I see that You have created all things to be stable, it gives me more confidence to ask You for the gift of poise. For what I ask, You delight to give. I am so deeply thankful. Amen.

EVERYTHING IS ON OUR SIDE

For reading and meditation – Isaiah 26:1–12

You will keep in perfect peace him whose
mind is steadfast, because he trusts in you. (v 3)

'But why spend so much time on the physical universe? Ought
we not to skip over this and get down more quickly to the
more important spiritual issues?' someone might ask.

I know of no better answer than to use the words of Jesus: 'If I
have told you earthly things and you do not believe, how will you
believe if I tell you heavenly things?' (John 3:12 NKJV). The effort
we make to comprehend what goes on in the physical universe all
around us will enable us to understand more fully what goes on
in the unseen and mysterious world of the spirit and our inner
personality.

Our nervous system is so arranged that if it cannot change what
goes on outside us, it works to keep us inwardly stable and steady
and will not allow the outer to affect us harmfully.

The Christian way to serenity and poise

MAY 7

O Father, I realise that I ought to be walking the earth as a
conqueror. I am being sustained naturally and supernaturally.
Thank You, Father. Amen.

COLD-BLOODED CHRISTIANS

FOR READING AND MEDITATION – ROMANS 12:1–12

Don't let the world around you squeeze you into its own mould ...

(v 2 PHILLIPS)

There is convincing evidence that a living organism is designed by God so that poise and stability are achieved despite outward changes. On the hottest day of the year, our body temperature maintains itself at about 37 degrees Centigrade. Our system fights to maintain itself at its normal temperature. In the coldest weather, just below the outer levels of our skin, we are as warm as usual.

This mechanism of the body makes it possible for us to live and be active in different climates and over a range of temperatures.

Cold-blooded mammals, whose temperature matches that of their surroundings, move around easily only when the weather is warm. Some Christians take on the temperature of their surroundings – like these cold-blooded mammals. They are spiritually warm when others are warm and spiritually cold when others are cold. This is because they have lost their spiritual poise and need to be 'warmed up' by periodic conventions and conferences.

O God, save me from being spiritually cold-blooded. In Jesus' Name I pray. Amen.

WORLDLY PATHS TO POISE

FOR READING AND MEDITATION – JOHN 6: 53–69
... Lord, to whom shall we go? You have
the words of eternal life. (v 68 NKJV)

The various philosophies that circulate the world are an attempt to do in the spiritual realm what nature does in the physical realm – namely, to provide for stability and poise in the midst of life's changing circumstances. This common goal goes under different words, such as peace, tranquillity, a quiet mind, harmony, integration, self-realisation or inner unity.

The approach of stoicism, for example, began with the Greeks, and was an attempt to harden the spirit so that it would match itself with hard and difficult circumstances.

This attempt has one fatal defect – the spirit becomes so hard that it cannot bend. And sometimes, because it cannot bend, it breaks. I have met many people in my time who thought they could get through life by adopting the attitudes of the Stoics, but I have seen their spirits become so brittle that they easily break.

🐾 *Gracious Father, help me not to approach life from a stoical standpoint, for then I will be brittle and breakable. Amen.*

MORE ABOUT STOICISM

FOR READING AND MEDITATION – PROVERBS 3:11–26

Her ways are ways of pleasantness, and all her paths are peace.

(v 17 NKJV)

The Stoics in their attempts to find inner serenity and poise, set out to achieve tranquillity by shutting out of the heart such things as love, compassion and pity. But to shut out love and pity is to shut out life. Those who follow this path strangle themselves to death searching for inner calm.

In one country I visited I commented to my host that I couldn't understand why the shops were so beautifully clean but the streets so unbearably dirty. 'Ah,' said my host, 'that is because the shops belong to the men and their families; the streets don't belong to anybody.'

They didn't see it as their responsibility. Any attempt to gain poise by refusing to face up to responsibility is not the Christian way. It produces the kind of person who cares only what happens to him and little or nothing about what happens to others. And that is fatal.

My Father, keep me ever walking in your paths, I pray. Only your ways are ways of peace. Amen.

POISE – AT THE EXPENSE OF INVOLVEMENT

FOR READING AND MEDITATION – ROMANS 12:9–21

Share the happiness of those who are happy,
and the sorrow of those who are sad. (v 15 PHILLIPS)

Another ineffective way of achieving inner poise is the way of mysticism.

The first time I visited India, I was struck with the number of people I saw sitting alone in the middle of a field or on the side of the road with their eyes closed. 'Most of them are Vedantists and they are affirming themselves to be Brahma, or God. Brahma is pure spirit, without bonds, without relationships and without attachment to anyone,' my host said.

'My guess is that they never get involved in changing things around them or feel any indignation over wrongs and injustices,' I said to my host.' 'That is precisely correct,' said my host.

The way of mysticism is the way of non-involvement. It seeks to find release from conflict by withdrawal. Christianity does not offer a way around conflict – it offers a way through.

☞ *My Father and my God, save me from building on falsehoods, for I know they will only collapse in the end. Amen.*

DOES GOD WILL EVIL?

Good and upright is the LORD; therefore he
instructs sinners in his ways. (v 8)

Another ineffective way of finding spiritual serenity and poise
is the religion of Islam. It believes that everything that happens to you is the will of God, so you should bend under it and
accept it as such.

Christians will see at once that Islam contains a kernel of truth,
but it also contains a dangerous untruth. If everything that happens is the will of God, then God must accept responsibility for all
the sin and suffering that is in the world. But how can a God of
love and righteousness actually will evil?

God, in making us free agents, is involved in the way things
have turned out in the world but any obligation God may have
had has been met and discharged at the cross. There everything
that fell upon man as a direct result of the misuse of his freedom,
fell upon Him. He bore what we should have borne and suffered
what we should have suffered.

Father, your will is for our highest interest – always. I am so
thankful. Amen.

DO SECURITIES SECURE?

FOR READING AND MEDITATION – MATTHEW 6:19–34

Do not store up for yourselves treasures on earth ... (v 19)

Some people attempt to find inner serenity and poise by acquiring material possessions. Those who follow this way adopt the attitude – become inwardly secure through outer securities. Plug up all possible cracks in your life through which poverty or hardship may come and make yourself secure by material possessions.

It is true that worry and concern about material things do affect us and material possessions can bring a sense of security. Material security can add greatly to one's peace of mind – up to a point. Beyond that, it is a false hope.

Those who pin their hopes for inner peace and poise on material security are building their nest too low. The floods may reach it.

My father's words, 'Money is a universal passport for everything but happiness, and a passport everywhere but to heaven,' have helped me make God and not gold my goal.

The Christian way to serenity and poise

MAY 13

☙ *O God, when I see men and women seeking for securities that cannot secure, help me put my confidence and trust wholly in You. In Jesus' Name. Amen.*

THE PURSUIT OF PLEASURE?

… In your presence is fullness of joy; at your
right hand are pleasures for evermore. (v 11 NKJV)

Hedonism, or the pleasure principle, is another ineffective answer to the question: 'How do I find inner serenity and poise?'

There is a sense in which it is quite legitimate to experience
pleasure, but the crux of the matter is how we go about getting
that pleasure. If we pursue pleasure itself, then we are on the
wrong track. Pleasure and happiness – that is, real pleasure and
happiness – are by-products; pursue them as an end in themselves
and they will burst like a bubble in your hands.

The pleasure principle, when pursued for its own sake, brings
unpleasurable regrets, disillusionments and hangovers. Those who
experience inner poise are those who give little or no attention to
their own happiness, but seek the happiness and welfare of others.
They lose their lives and find them.

🐾 *Gracious Father, save me from pursuing pleasure for its own
sake. Help me never to forget that it is always a by-product. When
I seek You, pleasure will seek me. Amen.*

KNOW THYSELF

For reading and meditation – Philippians 3:1–16

That I may know him and the power
of his resurrection ... (v 10 NKJV)

Another way men take in order to gain inner poise and serenity
is the way of self-knowledge. The ancient Greek saying, 'Know
thyself', contains a modicum of truth but it depends on what one
does with it and how one uses it.

Psychoanalysis which lays bare the depths and enables people to
understand what is going on inside them has contributed much,
but it can never produce the kind of inner serenity and poise which
the New Testament speaks about. Some disrupted people have
been picked to pieces in psychoanalysis but have not been properly
put together again.

Unless people can be put back together so that they function according to the principle of love for God and others, then all they have
to concentrate on is themselves. And the self that does not know God
can never know itself. It is like a dog chasing its own tail.

*O Father, I cannot truly know myself until I know You. Keep my
gaze ever fixed on You. For your own dear Name's sake. Amen.*

The Christian way to serenity and poise

NO HEAVEN WITHOUT CHRIST

For reading and meditation – Psalm 73:12–28

Whom have I in heaven but you? And there is none upon
earth that I desire besides you. (v 25 NKJV)

Some Christians rely for inner poise more on Christian truths
or concepts than on Christ Himself. Christ, and Christ alone,
must be the source of our inner serenity and poise.

Some Christians rely for inner poise on the prospect that one
day they will get to heaven, where all injustices will be corrected
and all wrongs put right. This is the concept that underlies most
(not all) of the Negro spirituals.

Now there is nothing wrong with these ideas, providing they are
secondary to Christ and not ahead of Him. You see, it is perilously
possible for a Christian truth or concept to take the place of Christ
in our hearts, and whenever that happens, God becomes greatly
grieved. We must allow nothing, absolutely nothing, no matter how
fine and noble it may be, to replace Christ as the centre and source
of our inner serenity and poise.

*O Father, help me to be a Christ-centred person, for only then
can I be a poised person. Amen.*

HEAVEN TO GO TO HEAVEN IN

For reading and meditation – Colossians 1:15–29

… the glorious riches of this mystery, which
is Christ in you, the hope of glory. (v 27)

If we rest on the future prospect of heaven as our source for serenity and poise, then we are resting on something outside of ourselves. Inner serenity and poise comes primarily through looking
to Christ and not to some future event, however good and glorious
the prospect might be.

In order to maintain our spiritual poise we need a continuing
realisation – something that holds us securely on the inside. Only
the living Christ dwelling in our hearts by the power of the Holy
Spirit can achieve that. No future can guarantee the present; the
present must guarantee the future.

After all, heaven is what it is because Jesus is who He is. In Jesus
we have a heaven here on earth and a heaven awaiting us in the
future. We have heaven to go to heaven in.

Lord Jesus Christ, because I have You, I have the future now.
Let this fact enable me to live above the possibility of fatal shake
and shock. Amen.

GETTING STRONGER AS WE GO

FOR READING AND MEDITATION – PSALM 84:1–12

Blessed is the man whose strength is in you, whose heart is set on
pilgrimage … They go from strength to strength … (vv 5–7 NKJV)

Paul said: 'Fight the good fight of faith' (1 Tim 6:12).

The word 'faith' depicts inner calm in the midst of struggle.
And notice also, it is described as a good fight. A fight that makes
you tense and strained is not a good fight; it is a bad fight. It leaves
you exhausted and drained. The Christian fight, being a 'fight of
faith', means that you struggle without your strength being
sapped, and fight without getting faint. Indeed, the very struggle
provides a deeper poise and serenity. The strength of the struggle
gets into you.

The idea of the Christian life as a ceaseless struggle which leaves
us strained and drained is not true. Unlike the ancient Israelites, we
don't have to push on to the next fountain – we have one continually bubbling up within.

The Christian way to serenity and poise

🖙 *O Father, I am grateful that I shall never thirst, for the source
of my supply is within. Hallelujah!*

POISE TO THE N^TH DEGREE

FOR READING AND MEDITATION – LUKE 4:1–15

Then Jesus returned in the power of
the Spirit to Galilee … (v 14 NKJV)

Did our Lord, when He was here on earth, manifest this deep serenity and poise about which we are speaking? Look at the very first picture we have of Him in the gospels at the age of twelve. (Luke 2:49). What serenity and confidence – He knew He was in the right place doing the right thing at the right time.

The second picture shows that same inner tranquillity. Led by the Holy Spirit into the wilderness to be tempted by the devil, He not only goes in with poise but comes out of it in the same way. He 'returned in the power of the Spirit'.

Here was poise to its nth degree. Here is the authentic spirit that could endure struggle and yet come through with inner power and poise. That which was intended to weaken Him ended only in strengthening Him.

The Christian way to serenity and poise

MAY 19

🐦 *O Father, now I see even more clearly what spiritual poise is all about – a spirit that meets everything and masters everything. Teach me to be like Jesus. Amen.*

DID JESUS LOSE HIS POISE?

FOR READING AND MEDITATION – JOHN 14:15–27

Peace I leave with you; my peace I give you ... (v 27)

There are those who claim that on several occasions in the New Testament, our Lord lost his inner serenity and poise. Can this really be true? If it is we are sunk, for how can He hold us calm and steady if He failed in this respect Himself?

Do these several occasions mean there is a fly in the ointment of Jesus' serenity and poise? I do not believe so. A living being maintains its stability only if it is excitable and capable of modifying itself according to external stimuli and adjusting the response to the situation.

This apparent contradiction contains a powerful spiritual truth. Things are stable because they are modifiable – the slight instability is the necessary condition for stability. In other words, without disturbance, there can be no stability. The things that upset us actually work to set us up.

Blessed Lord Jesus, I see that even as You drew near to the cross, You had sufficient peace and poise. Fill my heart with that same power this day. Amen.

ARE YOU GROWING?

FOR READING AND MEDITATION – 2 PETER 3:8–18

But grow in the grace and knowledge of
our Lord and Saviour Jesus Christ. (v 18)

Poise is not necessarily freedom from disturbance, complete absence of inner tension and concern or without feeling any inner pain or hurt. It is a denial of reality if we fail to understand this.

On all the five occasions we have touched on, Jesus was obviously troubled and perturbed, and because He was human as well as divine, He reacted to them with deep concern. He experienced a troubled mind, but passed through it to the tranquil mind.

Christ appeared to have a short adjustment period to disturbing events, and based on this, we can measure our spiritual growth and likeness to Christ by the length of time we take to recover our spiritual poise when something happens to upset us.

How is your spiritual adjustment period? Long or short? Do you recover more quickly from upsets now than you did a few years ago? If so, then you are growing.

O Father, help me to come out quickly on the other side of every calamity. In Jesus' Name I pray. Amen.

THE MASTER'S POISE – AVAILABLE

FOR READING AND MEDITATION – ACTS 2:14–36

But Peter, standing up with the eleven, raised his voice ...
(v 14 NKJV)

Was our Lord able to pass on to his followers the inner serenity and poise which He Himself possessed when He was
here on earth? The Day of Pentecost proves an unqualified 'Yes'.

The once faltering Simon Peter now stands up and charges the
nation with Christ's murder. His inner serenity and poise are so
overwhelming that he immediately attracts the attention of the
great crowd in Jerusalem and succeeds in bringing thousands of
them through the door of repentance into the kingdom of God.

What made this weakest of disciples such a positive and powerful herald of truth? Some think it was the resurrection of Jesus
that gave the disciples confidence and power.

But it was the coming of the Holy Spirit. No amount of good
information could produce transformation and give them the strength
and power they needed to face the days ahead. Only the Holy Spirit
could impart to them the Master's inner power and poise.

🕊 *O Father, come and flood me with your power and poise. In
Jesus' Name. Amen.*

NO SPIRIT – NO POISE

FOR READING AND MEDITATION – ACTS 4:1–13

... By what power or by what name have you done this? (v 7 NKJV)

Prior to the Day of Pentecost, the disciples were vacillating in their allegiance to Christ. They were not spiritually stabilised and their output and achievements were meagre. Their possession of serenity and poise was occasional and intermittent, even though Christ was physically present with them. There can be little doubt that whatever the disciples possessed prior to Pentecost, the life within them functioned feebly.

Then something happened. A divine reinforcement took place. The key was the coming of the Spirit. Only the Holy Spirit could impart to the early disciples the power and poise which Christ demonstrated to them when He was with them on earth. It was the key then and it is the key now. No Spirit – no poise. It is as simple as that.

O God, I see that without the Holy Spirit, my resources are outside me – only the Spirit can bring them within. I open my heart, dear Father, to experience still more of your Spirit. Flood me with your power. Amen.

NOT JUST FOR SOME – FOR ALL

FOR READING AND MEDITATION – ACTS 6:12–15; 7:54–60

But Stephen, full of the Holy Spirit, looked up to heaven
and saw the glory of God … (7:55)

The early disciples would not have become the poised and radiant followers of Christ, had it not been for the coming of the
Holy Spirit.

The direct impact of the coming of the Holy Spirit upon the
lives of the first disciples could be seen in his later disciples also.

The account, when Stephen was being stoned to death, says: 'His
face was like the face of an angel.'

Later Stephen prayed: 'Lord, do not hold this sin against them.'
This is poise and this is power. He responded to his death in the
same way that Jesus had responded to his death – by praying for
his murderers. It is clear, then, that even though Stephen was not
part of the original group of disciples, the same power and poise
that Jesus had demonstrated was evident in him also.

🖝 *O Father, hold me from within, in the same way that You held
your servant Stephen. In Jesus' Name I pray. Amen.*

THE DIVIDING LINE

When the day of Pentecost came,
they were all together in one place. (v 1)

The coming of the Holy Spirit into the inner lives of Christ's early disciples gave them a power and a poise comparable to nothing ever before seen on earth. He brought with Him all the benefits of Christ's redemptive death on Calvary and made it possible for us to have the character of Christ transplanted into the depths of our beings. Far too many try to live out the Christian life in the energy of the flesh.

If you draw a line through the pages of the New Testament, you will find on one side those who are spiritually sterile and inadequate, on the other side those who are filled with spiritual poise and power.

If you have not allowed Him entrance to your inner being, then you are living on the wrong side of the line. Admit your weakness and inadequacy and step over the line.

The Christian way to serenity and poise

MAY 25

O Father, I don't want to live a dull Christian life – I want to live a dynamic one. Help me, dear Lord. In Jesus' Name. Amen.

TWELVE POWERLESS DISCIPLES

For reading and meditation – ACTS 19:1–10
And when Paul had laid hands on them, the Holy Spirit
came upon them … (v 6 NKJV)

When Paul arrived in Ephesus, he sensed that some of the
believers there lacked power and adequacy, so he said to
them: 'Did you receive the Holy Spirit when you believed?'

Apollos, the spiritual leader of the twelve men in that group, was
an eloquent man, well versed in the Scriptures, but he knew only
the outer baptism, not the inner baptism. Compare these twelve
disciples at Ephesus with the twelve disciples at Pentecost. The
Ephesian disciples simply turned over the pages of the Scriptures,
the other disciples 'turned the world upside down'.

Prior to Pentecost, the twelve disciples were weak and dispirited –
following Pentecost, they were radiant and exhilarated.

Had the Holy Spirit not come, Christianity would have been the
kind that would have kept the disciples behind closed doors – fearful, apprehensive and inadequate.

*Father, I see that without the Holy Spirit, I am a flickering
torch instead of a flaming torch. I would be alight with You, re-
inforced by You at the depths. Amen.*

A BIBLICAL CAMEO

FOR READING AND MEDITATION – EPHESIANS 1:3–14

... in whom also, having believed, you were sealed
with the Holy Spirit of promise. (v 13 NKJV)

The power of the Holy Spirit is of supreme importance in the
Christian faith. Jesus was conceived, anointed, went into the
wilderness by the direction of the Spirit (Matt 4:1) and came out
in his power.

Jesus began his ministry by announcing that the Spirit of the
Lord was upon Him and cast out evil spirits by the Spirit

He was offered up as a sacrifice, was raised from the dead and
on the Day of Pentecost baptised one hundred and twenty of his
followers in the Holy Spirit.

We are transformed into God's image by the Holy Spirit. The
Spirit guides us into all truth and we are strengthened by the Holy
Spirit in our inner man.

And it is He who develops within us the character of Christ
which we know as 'the fruit of the Spirit' (Gal 5:22–23).

The Christian way to serenity and poise

🖝 *O Father, help me to see the Holy Spirit as a doctrine but also
as a dynamic. Grant it, dear Lord – in ever increasing measure.
Amen.*

OUR LORD'S LAST WORDS

FOR READING AND MEDITATION – ACTS 1:1–14

… wait for the promise of the Father … (v 4 RSV)

The supreme reason why the Holy Spirit came at Pentecost, was to make the nature and character of Christ available to his followers. The Welsh theologian, Dr Cynddylan Jones, said: 'The doctrine of the Holy Spirit is the intensification and extension of the doctrine of Christ within.'

Our Lord had said many powerful things to his disciples – love your enemies, be the servant of all in order to be the greatest of all, lose your life if you want to find it, and so on. However, last impressions are usually lasting impressions, so what were our Lord's last statements to his disciples? Did He pick out one of them and give it special emphasis? No, He said: ' Wait for the promise of the Father.' If they had missed this, they would have missed the central point of redemption. For the Holy Spirit is the applied point of redemption – continuing redemption in the depth of our being.

O Father, take over my 'within'. In Christ's Name I ask it. Amen.

STAY IN THE CITY

FOR READING AND MEDITATION – LUKE 24:44–53

... wait in the city ... (v 49 MOFFAT)

Jesus commanded the disciples to stay in the city. He wanted them to discover right away that the same serenity and poise which carried Him through his own ordeal would also be theirs – in the same city where He had been crucified.

Why in the 'city'? I suggest that if they had received the Spirit in the solitude, they might have had a lurking doubt as to whether the resources they had been given would work in the stress and strain of a city atmosphere. See the point? If this new power which was to operate in them could operate in the city of Jerusalem where Christ had met with such hostility, then it could operate anywhere.

The Holy Spirit is continuing redemption in our inner being. Apart from the Holy Spirit, redemption is outside of us – in history in the historical Jesus. But in and through the Holy Spirit, the historical becomes the experiential.

The Christian way to serenity and poise

🖛 *O God, I am so thankful that, empowered by the Holy Spirit, I can face the most difficult situation. Amen.*

SUCCESS AT THE POINT OF FAILURE

FOR READING AND MEDITATION – ACTS 4:23–33
And with great power the apostles gave witness to
the resurrection of the Lord Jesus ... (v 33 NKJV)

Another reason why Christ commanded his disciples to 'wait in the city' was to help them understand, right from the start, that the power and poise which they would receive at the descent of the Holy Spirit were able to hold them fast in the most difficult situations. But something else about the city worth considering is – it was here that the disciples had so signally failed.

In the hour of crisis, the disciples had forsaken their Lord and appeared not to have made any attempt to assist Him. What they had done must have caused deep feelings of inferiority and inadequacy to rise up within them. Jesus would wipe out those feelings of inferiority by making them a success in the very place where they had been the biggest failures.

Father, I see that I do not have to concern myself about how to escape from my problems; I need only concern myself how to encompass them with your power. In Christ's Name I pray. Amen.

THE OLD BECOMES THE NEW

FOR READING AND MEDITATION – REVELATION 21:1–7

... Behold, I make all things new ... (v 5 NKJV)

Religion is sometimes used by people as a means of escaping from reality, a dodging of issues, a drugging of the emotions. True Christianity, however, enables us to look whatever comes fully in the face and deal with it, no matter how hard and difficult it may be. Christ is not an anaesthetic – He is an answer. He does not drug us or dupe us, but imparts to us the power by which we can meet everything with confidence and poise.

When the disciples found out that they had an inner power that enabled them to stand up and call the crowds that thronged the streets of Jerusalem to repentance – the crowds whose hands were red with the blood of their Master – then they knew they had an answer which led through life and not around it.

The Christian way to serenity and poise

MAY 31

O God, in You I can bounce back. Deliver me from the Jeru-salem of my failures and fears and make it a new Jerusalem – a Jerusalem of joy. In Jesus' Name. Amen.

WHO CAN SOUND THE DEPTHS?

For reading and meditation – 1 Corinthians 2:1–12

... for the Holy Spirit searches diligently ... even sounding
the profound and bottomless things of God ... (v 10 amp)

The actions of the Holy Spirit in the life of a believer are many
and varied, but I want to focus now on the way in which He
unifies the conscious and the unconscious.

We know a lot about the conscious mind, but the most powerful
work the Holy Spirit can effect in our lives is in the unconscious.

What goes on there is determinative and influential. David Sea-
bury says: 'All of our real thinking and three-quarters of our mental activity transpires below the surface of our awareness and only
comes to the surface as the time of active use arrives'.

The Holy Spirit, He who sounds the profound and bottomless
depths of God, is able to fathom the hidden depths of man.

*O Father, I am so thankful that your Spirit knows me better
than I know myself. This means You can help me, not just at the
surface of my life, but in the hidden depths. Amen.*

THOSE DARK MYSTERIOUS DEPTHS

FOR READING AND MEDITATION – GENESIS 1:1–16

... and the Spirit of God was moving over
the surface of the waters. (v 2 NASB)

One of the most powerful things the Spirit does in the area of
human personality is (so I believe) in the unconscious.

If our religion deals with only a small part of the personality –
the conscious – we give ourselves to something that may look ap-
pealing but lacks the power to bring about deep inner change.
About one-tenth of the mind is conscious and like an iceberg about
nine-tenths is largely in the submerged portion of our being.

I am using the word *unconscious* rather than 'subconscious',
because the unconscious is much deeper than the subconscious
and is shrouded in darkness and mystery. Can the Spirit reach
into these dark depths of the personality? I say – He can. He who
brought cosmos out of chaos will not be baffled by the dark con-
tents of our inner being.

The Christian way to serenity and poise

JUNE 2

🖎 *My Father and my God, I need cleansing and coordination
of my inner being. I want to be made whole. Amen.*

THE LIGHT OF TRANSFORMATION

FOR READING AND MEDITATION – LUKE 11:29–36

If therefore your whole body is full of light, with no
dark part in it, it shall be wholly illumined … (v 36 NASB)

The part from which things are fairly easily retrieved, for example, when we remember a person's name, an event or a situation, is the subconscious, the area between the conscious and the
unconscious. What goes on deeper down in the unconscious is not
so easily retrievable, for, like a deep, dark cellar in which there is
little or no light, it is easy to stumble and lose one's way.

The Holy Spirit does not lose his way in the unconscious. He who
brought light into the material universe is well able to lighten the
darkness of our inner being. This can it be scripturally supported,
for the verse before us tells us that the Gospel of Jesus Christ offers
an inner life with 'no part dark'. And: 'Where the Spirit of the Lord
is, there is freedom' (2 Cor 3:17 RSV).

*O God, I want so much that my inner being should have 'no
part dark'. Help me, my Father. Amen.*

ARE YOU GETTING NOWHERE?

FOR READING AND MEDITATION – MATTHEW 23:25–39

Woe to you, teachers of the law and Pharisees …
You clean the outside of the cup and dish, but inside
they are full of greed and self-indulgence. (v 25)

The quest for light and illumination in the unconscious can be scripturally supported. About the verse that is before us, Kunkel says: 'Depth psychology (i.e. the study and application of therapy to the unconscious) was never more accurately described than in these words of Jesus.'

Most of the inner conflicts we experience arise from the fact that there is disunity between the conscious and the unconscious. The conscious mind wants one thing, while the unconscious wants another. Take this verse: 'For I delight in the law of God, in my inmost self, but I see in my members another law at war with the law of my mind and making me captive to the law of sin which dwells in my members' (Rom 7:22–23 RSV).

Hence many Christian lives are at a standstill, for the unconverted unconscious cancels out the converted conscious. The result? We get nowhere.

O Father, I don't want to spend my life getting nowhere. Make me a united person. In Jesus' Name I pray. Amen.

AN EVANGELIST WITH A PROBLEM

FOR READING AND MEDITATION – JEREMIAH 17:5–14

The heart is deceitful above all things … Who can
understand it? I the LORD search the heart … (vv 9–10)

A young evangelist told his counsellor that ever since he had
approached his girlfriend and asked her to marry him, he had
not been able to eat anything with wheat in it.

The counsellor found that the real reason why he could not go
through with the marriage ceremony and kept finding a reason
to call it off was that he was unconsciously holding the view that
marriage and being an evangelist were incompatible.

It was pointed out to him that the connection between being
unable to assimilate marriage into his life and his inability to assimilate wheat into his physical system were closely connected. He
had transferred his spiritual problem to a physical object. To experience inner serenity and poise, we must know unity between the
conscious and the unconscious.

*My Father and my God, I see that unless You enlighten me, I
will never be able to understand myself. Give me your light and
illumination. In Jesus' Name I pray. Amen.*

UNREDEEMED DESIRES

For reading and meditation – Romans 7:13–25

O wretched man that I am! Who will deliver
me from this body of death? (v 24 NKJV)

Any conflict between conscious and unconscious can give an undertone to life of unhappiness and frustration and robs us of inner serenity and poise. Sometimes the depths are revealed in strange ways.

In the town where Charles Holman was born lived a woman and her daughter, both of whom walked in their sleep.

During their waking hours they lived on the polite but repressed level of the conscious, but deep resentments festered underneath. Those hidden resentments drained their lives of real joy.

How many of us, who profess to follow Christ, are trying to divide our loyalties between mutually exclusive things? We profess to have Christian desires and Christian longings, and yet deep within are strongly entrenched desires and longings that have never been redeemed. We believe in God with the top of our mind, but deep down, we are committed to our own self-centred ways.

The Christian way to serenity and poise

O Father, I open all to you. Cleanse me in the secret places and in the hidden depths. I ask it in Jesus' Name. Amen.

GOD AT WORK

FOR READING AND MEDITATION – PHILIPPIANS 1:1–11
Being confident of this, that he who began a good work
in you will carry it on to completion ... (v 6)

Unconscious desires can influence our conscious decisions and
our behaviour. A woman who was anxious to have children,
but was barren, always read the word *stock* as the word *stork*.
This happened against her conscious will and was caused by hidden and deeper instincts that influenced her wishes and desires.

A woman who had once signed her name to a document that
was fraudulently used, got cramp in her fingers whenever she
signed her name.

Many of our blunders and some of our forgetfulness is due to
unconscious tendencies conflicting with our conscious intentions.
All of life, conscious and unconscious, must be brought under a
single control, directed toward a single end with all of its forces
harmonised, or else life is frustrated. The power and redemption
must be there as continuously as the unconscious itself. Remind
yourself that God is continuously working to make you whole.

O Father, I take comfort from the text that is before me. I am
deeply thankful. Amen.

THE GOOD STORE

FOR READING AND MEDITATION – MATTHEW 12:25–37

The good man brings good out of his good store ... (v 35 MOFFAT)

The unconscious is the residing place of many of our driving instincts and urges. Like other aspects of our being, the unconscious has the potential of being used for good or for evil. God provided for what today's text describes as 'the good store'.

This is how it works: every time we meditate on a text of Scripture, every time we think a good thought, every time we do a good deed, every time we focus on a right attitude, this then drops into our unconscious mind and thus becomes a part of that 'good store' which is being built up within.

The 'good store' in the unconscious takes over in a conscious crisis and provides us with the inner resources we need to make the right conscious decisions. Our 'good store' helps us to come up with goodness.

The Christian way to serenity and poise

JUNE 8

✎ *Lord, I see that a positive as well as a negative side to my unconscious is your beneficent way to keep me on the road of goodness. Thank You, dear Father. Amen.*

BEING HELD TO GOODNESS

For reading and meditation – Psalm 119:1–16
Your word I have hidden in my heart,

that I might not sin against you. (v 11 NKJV)

Every good thought and every good deed drops into the unconscious mind and becomes part of that 'good store' which is being built up within. This is why it is so important to develop the habit of daily exposing your mind to the word of God, for what you read drops deep inside you and is laid up on the shelves of the 'good store', ready for use whenever it is needed.

The 'good store' holds us to goodness by disposition and habit. It becomes second nature to us to do the right thing, say the right word or take the right attitude. In this way, the unconscious can work beneficently and to our advantage.

In every one of us there is a definite bent towards evil drives. But they can be surrendered to the Holy Spirit and brought into unity to one end – the glory of God.

The Christian way to serenity and poise

JUNE 9

O God, I am so thankful for this insight that I was not designed to function with my conscious and unconscious at variance. Amen.

MORE COMFORTABLE
WHEN UNHAPPY

FOR READING AND MEDITATION – PSALM 139:1–24

Search me, O God, and know my heart;
test me and know my anxious thoughts. (v 23)

We will never know inner serenity and poise unless we take the steps that are necessary to bring about the unifying of the conscious and unconscious.

In a seminar I have said to people: 'How many of you have ever experienced a relationship in which everything seems to be going wonderfully but for some reason, you feel very uncomfortable about it and become withdrawn or even depressed. Then you find yourself doing something to provoke an argument after which you feel unhappy, but for some strange reason you feel more comfortable with the unhappiness than you did with the happiness. How many have ever felt like that?'

It's astonishing how many raise their hands in response. This is due to the fact that what we want with the conscious is not what we want with the unconscious, and in any battle between the conscious and the unconscious, the unconscious usually wins.

🐚 *O Father, continue to dig deeply into my life, for I want to be fully whole. Amen.*

HAPPINESS ANXIETY

FOR READING AND MEDITATION – 2 CHRONICLES 25:1–16

He did what was right in the eyes of the Eternal,
but not with an undivided mind. (v 2 MOFFAT)

'Happiness anxiety', described as 'the anxiety a person feels whenever they become happy', is known to affect millions of people.

This is how it works: if a person believes deep down in their unconscious that they have no right to be happy or that they do not deserve to be happy, then no matter how much they long to be happy with their conscious mind, the unconscious, being stronger and more powerful than the conscious, will eventually get its way.

Usually the person has an unconscious desire to fail. But why should a person want to fail? Because they can handle failure better than they can handle success. Does that sound strange and bizarre to you? Much stranger things go on in the human heart. That is why we need a salvation. And such a salvation we have – in Christ.

O Father, take my hand in yours and lead me through this maze so that I can find deliverance from these inner contradictions. In Christ's peerless and precious Name. Amen.

SPIRITUAL SABOTAGE

FOR READING AND MEDITATION – JOB 3:20–26

What I feared has come upon me;
what I dreaded has happened to me. (v 25)

A young girl once came to me in a church which I was pastoring and said: 'Will you please pray with me that God will give me a Christian boyfriend?' It appeared to be a sincere request and one which I felt I could give myself to in prayer.

As I began to pray, I remembered that the girl's attitudes and behaviour toward members of the opposite sex were such that it would put any eligible young man off. I stopped praying and pointed this out to her. She confessed that she had a history of being rejected by male figures in her family. Rejection was the thing she was most familiar with and had come to expect.

Her unconscious was sabotaging her conscious desires. She surrendered the depths to God, learned through counselling how to accept herself and went on to marry a fine young minister.

☞ *Gracious Master, I don't want to walk through life with a Trojan horse within, ready to betray me at my weakest moment. Help me. In Jesus' Name. Amen.*

AN UNCONSCIOUS DESIRE TO FAIL

FOR READING AND MEDITATION – EPHESIANS 4:17–32
Get rid of all bitterness, rage and anger, brawling and slander,
along with every form of malice. (v 31)

Not just our prayer lives – every other aspect of our lives also,
can easily be sabotaged unless there is unity between the conscious and the unconscious.

Many years ago a young man came to see me to discuss his repeated failure in examinations. There appeared to be no explanation for this. While praying with him, the Spirit prompted me to say: 'Deep down in your heart, your desire to fail is stronger than your desire to succeed. Why should that be?

Soon the whole problem was unravelled. The young man had been brought up by parents who had put tremendous pressure on him to pass his examinations, saying such things as, 'If you don't pass, we won't love you.' Inside him this pressure had produced great resentment which he had repressed. He surrendered the resentment to God and went on to pass his next examination.

O God my Father, take my consciousness and my unconsciousness and let them dance together to your music. Blessed be your Name. Amen.

THE NORMAL CHRISTIAN LIFE

FOR READING AND MEDITATION – ROMANS 8:1–17

For the law of the Spirit of life in Christ Jesus has made
me free from the law of sin and death. (v 2 NKJV)

Now that we have seen something of how the unconscious
works and how strongly influential it is, we look at some of
the ways people take to deal with this mysterious part of their
personality.

Some people use suppression – in psychological terms – as a
depository for the things they are tired of looking at or have no
present use for. If the things put in the spare room or cupboard
are of such a nature that a person never wants to see them again
and nails up the door, then this would be repression.

Here Christianity and the best insights of psychology are one
– both teach that suppression and repression are harmful to the
personality.

Normal Christianity must be viewed from the perspective of
Romans 8: 'The Spirit of life in Christ Jesus has made me free
from the law of sin and death' (Rom 8:2 NKJV).

The Christian way to serenity and poise

🌾 *Father, thank You for reminding me that You have provided
for success in Christian living. Amen.*

KEEP OFF! HIGH VOLTAGE!

FOR READING AND MEDITATION – 1 JOHN 1:1–10

If we confess our sins, he is faithful and just and will
forgive us our sins and purify us from all unrighteousness. (v 9)

Incomplete repentance or routine confession is another way used
by people but which does not get to the roots of the problem.
This happens when we use the 'confessional' as a way of trying to
get forgiveness for wrong behaviour while still holding on to the
wrong underlying attitudes that prompted the behaviour.

Both the sinner and the absolver live in an unconscious agreement never to touch the poisonous roots. Keep off! High voltage!
This is why two thousand years of confessional practice have failed
to discover the unconscious.

Real confession takes place when we open up our whole being
to God, conscious and unconscious, the lower reaches as well as
the upper reaches. Confessing wrong actions without confessing
the underlying attitudes is about as helpful as continually sweep-
ing away a cobweb and letting the spider remain.

JUNE 15 | *The Christian way to serenity and poise*

🕊 *Father, You are probing deep. Help me understand that You
are seeking, not just to make me better but to make me well. Amen.*

CONTROLLED EXPRESSION

FOR READING AND MEDITATION – GALATIANS 5:13–26

... live by the Spirit, and you will not gratify
the desires of the sinful nature. (v 16)

Some of the more dominant instincts and drives that swirl around in the unconscious are: the drive for power – or, as it is sometimes called, the self urge. Then there is the drive to find meaning and purpose, the herd instinct and many others. One drive that is extremely dominant within us is the drive for sensual pleasure.

It is important to realise that God is not interested in eradicating these natural drives and instincts. However, if the devices of suppression, repression and incomplete confession do not touch the problem of the unconscious, then what does? The answer is expression – expression that is under the control of the Holy Spirit.

Leslie Weatherhead, a man who had great insight into the personality said that when we adopt the methods of evasion and pretence, these forces then function at the depth of the personality at which they cannot be controlled.

☙ *O Father, tame these instincts and drives within me and harness them to the cause of your Kingdom. In Jesus' Name. Amen.*

THE MASTER'S VOICE

FOR READING AND MEDITATION – JOHN 1:1–14
Through him all things were made; without him
nothing was made that has been made. (v 3)

Our instincts and drives were originally designed to advance our personalities, but sin has twisted them and thus they have sent us into retreat. The divine strategy is not elimination but, as we said earlier – controlled expression. This happens when these instincts are taken over by God and are converted so that they can find their expression at a higher level. Now they can be fulfilled only when they are surrendered to God and his purposes.

If we surrender our drives to God, then they become 'life in Him'. We live abundantly – with inner serenity and poise. When we leave them to run themselves, they are death. They die themselves and they produce death in us. Outside of God there is nothing but death; inside of God there is nothing but life. Life knows its Master, and lives only when it hears and obeys the Master's voice.

🖎 *O God, I am so thankful that You are not just Lord, but Lord of all. Thank You my Father. Amen.*

LETTING NATURE CAPER

For reading and meditation – Hebrews 10:19–39

… the Spirit of grace. (v 29 nkjv)

In our text, the Holy Spirit is described as ' the Spirit of grace'. The Spirit applies grace in the place where it counts – in the depths, in the unconscious. The instincts in our unconscious cannot be eradicated and must not be repressed, but with the help of God they can be put behind the central purpose of our lives. Then they become a driving force rather than a draining force; the wild horses are tamed and harnessed to the tasks of the Kingdom.

After Pentecost the disciples weren't suppressing their instincts – they were expressing them. They were letting nature caper, because it was controlled by the Holy Spirit.

How devils must have trembled on that day when the Spirit was poured out. One preacher describes the demons saying to each other as they saw God about to give the promised Spirit on the Day of Pentecost: 'Hell help us! All heaven is about to break loose.'

The Christian way to serenity and poise

JUNE 18

🕊 *O Spirit of grace, I know in You I find not only redemption, but redirection. Thank You, dear Father. Amen.*

MARRED – BUT REMADE

FOR READING AND MEDITATION – EPHESIANS 2:1–10

… God, who is rich in mercy, made us alive with Christ
even when we were dead in transgressions … (vv 4–5)

I cannot stress enough that the drives and instincts that reside
within us are not corrupt in themselves – they are God-made
and God-ordained.

When however, we take them into our own hands and we become God, then that is the root of all sin. When that happens, life is
corrupted at the centre. The self becomes egotistical, sex becomes
sensuality, the herd instinct becomes the worldly mind, obeying
popular opinion. An abscess forms at the centre of our being, and
just as an abscessed tooth is likely to give you rheumatism and
other ailments, so an abscessed or corrupted self will bring other
aches and pains into the entire self. We give ourselves a pain.

We must lose our driving urges, lose them in a higher will and
then we find them again as self-expression.

O Father, You not only made me, but You are able to remake
me. Re-fashion me, dear Lord, into your glorious image. Amen.

THE TOUCH OF THE MASTER'S HAND

FOR READING AND MEDITATION – JEREMIAH 18:1–12

… so he made it again into another vessel, as it seemed
good to the potter to make. (v 4 NKJV)

We get rid of self-centredness by replacing it with God-centred-
ness; of our sexual drive and of the dominating herd drive
by surrendering it to God.

The strategy of the Spirit is not just to condemn our sinful inner
drives and desires, but to cleanse and consecrate them to the purposes of the Kingdom. The Holy Spirit cleanses away the wrong
attachments and motives and then consecrates those urges to supreme loyalty to God and service to man. Then they are drives that
drive forward into life.

We are able to love people more because we are no longer dom-
inated by them. Our hearts are free – to love. We make the satis-
fying discovery that instead of sex dominating us, it serves us. It
makes us more creative than ever before and adds a zest and sparkle
to our entire personality.

🖙 My Father and my God, help me to give myself to your perfect
will with complete abandon and complete joy. In Jesus' Name.
Amen.

SPECIAL AGENT

FOR READING AND MEDITATION – 1 THESSALONIANS 1:1–10

... our gospel came to you not simply with words, but also
with power, with the Holy Spirit and with deep conviction. (v 5)

What steps must we take in order that the Holy Spirit might
reside and preside in our unconscious?

The Spirit is the Trinity's 'special agent' for life and power and
wherever we see Him at work, we observe this particular and special emphasis. When we surrender to Christ, the Holy Spirit comes
into us to impart life to our dead spirit and bring about regenera-
tion (John 3:5).

Although it is true that every Christian has the Holy Spirit, the
Holy Spirit does not have every Christian. It is not enough to in-
vite Him in – He needs to be given complete control. Picture the
Christian life like marriage. There is an initial surrender and yet a
continuous surrender. It takes a long time to be married well, for
larger areas and deeper depths have to be brought into the marriage relationship.

*Father, I face the question now: I have the Holy Spirit but does
the Holy Spirit have me? Help me, my Father. Amen.*

YOUR CRY TRIGGERS GOD'S SUPPLY

FOR READING AND MEDITATION – PSALM 34:1–22

The eyes of the LORD are on the righteous and
his ears are attentive to their cry. (v 15)

Several months after my conversion to Christ, I experienced
some strange and fierce conflicts going on inside me. I went to
my pastor who counselled me along this line: 'At conversion the
conflicts were swept out of your conscious mind as the love of
Christ came in, but the instincts in your unconscious were just
cowed – they needed also to be brought under the sway of the
Spirit. These suppressed instincts are like the Chinese pirates who,
in olden days, used to hide in the hold of a vessel and then rose
up while the ship was on her voyage and tried to capture the
bridge, and with it the ship. Then, of course, a fight ensued.'

This graphic word picture helped me realise that I needed to let
the Spirit come into the depths as well. 'Your cry will trigger off
God's supply', my pastor told me.

The christian way to serenity and poise

O God, I cry – You supply. I believe it and rest upon it. In Jesus'
Name. Amen.

HOW MUCH MORE . . .

FOR READING AND MEDITATION – LUKE 11:1–13

… how much more will your Father in heaven
give the Holy Spirit to those who ask him! (v 13)

God is more eager to give you the fullness of his Spirit than
you are to receive.

Note the words – 'how much more'. Is there anything that a
loving parent would rather do than give a good gift to his child
– something that the child has longed for over a period of weeks
or months? Those of you who are parents must know something
of this feeling, but now multiply that feeling a million times and
you have just a faint idea of the eagerness that God has in relation
to giving you his Holy Spirit. Listen to the words again: 'how
much more'. The Holy Spirit is not something that God gives
grudgingly or sparingly – He yearns to give Him.

God has come a long way to give you his Holy Spirit. He burst
into the Upper Room at Pentecost and made Himself available to
all who receive Christ.

*O Father, come in all your fullness. In Jesus' Name I ask it.
Amen.*

UNMERITED INJUSTICE

FOR READING AND MEDITATION – 1 PETER 2:11–25

*... But if you suffer for doing good and you endure it,
this is commendable before God. (v 20)*

Why do bitterness and resentment arise in our hearts? Largely, it is our reaction to what we consider is an unmerited injustice. Many years ago, I was told – make up your mind that in a world of this kind, you are not going to escape injustice and unmerited pain. We say, 'Why should this happen to me?' Well, why not? Are you better than Jesus? Almost everything that can happen to a human being on this earth happened to Him.

The Christian life does not promise exemption from injustice and suffering, but it does promise power to make something good out of everything that happens. So forgive everyone who has ever hurt you – now. The Holy Spirit cannot come into the depths when the door to the unconscious is cluttered up with bitterness and resentment.

The Christian way to serenity and poise

☙ *O Father God, cleanse me now and help me forgive every injustice that has ever been done to me. I do so now, in and through Jesus' precious Name. Amen.*

OUR PRIME DIFFICULTY

So Jacob was left alone, and a man
wrestled with him till daybreak. (v 24)

When Jacob was about to meet the angered Esau, he sent
presents before him, hoping to save himself. There is much
of the Jacob in us. Adler was profoundly right when he said that
the ego urge is our prime difficulty in life and is at the basis of
most of our unhappiness. It is the one thing we clamour to hold
on to and own.

The recalcitrant Jacob must be subdued within us, even if it
means wrestling till the break of day. If, like many, you struggle
over the issue of self-surrender because you are not sure of yourself or sure of God, then heed these words of Sam Shoemaker, the
great American evangelist: 'Give as much of yourself that you know,
to as much of God that you know.' A beautifully worded and insightful statement. Put it to the test and act on it today.

The Christian way to serenity and poise

JUNE 25

🔖 *O Father, how true it is that I will give anything to You but
myself. But with your help I do so now. Amen.*

HOW TO ASK

FOR READING AND MEDITATION – MATTHEW 7:1–11

Ask and it will be given to you; seek and you will find;

knock and the door will be opened to you. (v 7)

When counselling people who have come to me saying they long for a deeper work of the Spirit in their lives, I have said to them: 'Have you asked God yourself for this?' When they say that they have, my next question is this: 'Tell me exactly what you asked for and how you asked for it.'

They used the right words and phrases, but there is more to asking than just words. True 'asking' involves an intensity of spirit – an inner desire that surpasses words. Words are the vehicle we use to express our thoughts, but the asking must come, not from the mind but from the spirit.

This is why Jesus drew attention to these three stages of intensity: ask, seek, knock. If you ask and don't receive, your asking needs to be wrapped around with deeper conviction and enthusiasm.

The Christian way to serenity and poise

O Father, help me crystallise my longings for the Holy Spirit until they become a burning focus in my life. In Jesus' Name. Amen.

THE ART OF RECEIVING

FOR READING AND MEDITATION – GALATIANS 3:1–14

Does God give you his Spirit … because you observe
the law, or because you believe what you heard? (v 5)

The promise of the Spirit is received through faith – that puts
the gift of the Spirit within the reach of all who will believe.
Anyone can accept a gift – even the smallest child. So become
childlike and take it. Don't look at yourself and your feelings –
look at Christ and his faithfulness. Let me remind you of a couple
of scriptures at this stage, for the Word of God is much more
powerful and effective than my words: ' He who calls you is faithful, who also will do it' (1 Thess 5:24 NKJV); ' Whatever things you
ask when you pray, believe that you receive them, and you will
have them' (Mark 11:24 NKJV).

Note, not 'you will receive them' but 'you receive them' – you
have them now on the basis of God's character which is behind
the promise of the Holy Spirit. Relax and receive.

*O Father, forgive me that my fears have strangled my faith.
Now fill me to overflowing. Amen.*

FOUNDATION FOR FAITH

For reading and meditation – 1 John 5:10–21

... this is the confidence that we have in him, that if we ask
anything according to his will, he hears us. (v 14 NKJV)

Faith is the basis on which we come to God and by which we
continue to receive from God.

There are five clear stages: (1) *Confidence:* confidence in the
character of God as seen in Christ. His word cannot fail because
his nature cannot change. (2) *Conversing:* 'if we ask anything'
– bringing our desires out of our hearts and not just musing on
them – conversing with Him about them. (3) *Condition:* 'according to his will' – knowing without any shadow of doubt that what
we ask is his purpose for us. (4) *Conviction:* we know that 'he
hears us, whatever we ask' – He hangs on every word we say. He
really does. (5) *Consequence:* I believe the condition is met – that
it is according to his will and that, as a consequence, I now receive
what I ask for.

O God, I am ready to be committed. Meet me, dear Father –
today. Amen.

The Christian way to serenity and poise

GIVING HIM THE REINS

FOR READING AND MEDITATION – ACTS 5:27–42
… the Holy Spirit, whom God has given
to those who obey him. (v 32)

The step to maintaining the presence of the Spirit in the unconscious is continuous obedience. The Holy Spirit must be always in control, for we maintain the Spirit's presence only as long as He retains control. When we take over and adopt an attitude of independence, He quietly steps aside and shuts off the sense of his power and presence until we decide to give Him the reins again.

Obedience means many things, but it means especially the daily discipline of reading his Word, prayer and the practice of good works. The Christian outlook is: surrender thyself, discipline thyself, obey another self – the Spirit of God. It is losing our life to find it again.

If you sow your life to the Spirit – that is, respond continually to the Spirit – then, as the sowed grain responds to the creative caresses of the earth, so you reap life. And how!

The Christian way to serenity and poise

JUNE 29

O Father God, take all my drives and instincts and put them under your schooling. Amen.

NOT THE END – THE BEGINNING

FOR READING AND MEDITATION – EPHESIANS 3:14–21

That he would grant you … to be strengthened with might
through his Spirit in the inner man. (v 16 NKJV)

We have seen that the Holy Spirit in possession of us, the
conscious and the unconscious, bringing about cleansing
and coordination, is the secret of remaining inwardly poised in an
unstable world.

This is the Christian way to inner serenity and poise.

Any religion that is just form will crash in the moment of crisis.
Many do not open themselves to a deep encounter with the Spirit,
and then are astonished that their faith does not hold them when
a crisis comes. Continue to open your being to the Holy Spirit, and
you will find that what you cultivate in the customary will be there
in the crisis in the form of inner serenity and poise.

Gracious and loving Father, as I come to the end of these
meditations, I am aware that this is not really the end – but the
beginning. I know that life is ahead of me, for life is within me.
Thank You, dear Father. Amen.

SERVING THE LORD BETTER

The words of Nehemiah son of Hacaliah: In the month
of Kislev … I was in the citadel of Susa. (v 1)

The main events of the book of Nehemiah took place in the
spring and summer of the year 445 B.C. During this period
Nehemiah made the journey from Susa, near the Persian Gulf, to
the city of Jerusalem in order to restore the city's ruined defences.

As a young man I was told that whatever career I chose for
myself, I would never be able to serve the Lord effectively until I
understood the principles set out in the book of Nehemiah. I
found that advice to be true. To enter into any career, whether in
the business world or the Christian ministry, without an understanding of the spiritual principles that hold life together is utter
foolishness. And many of those principles are illustrated most
powerfully in the story of Nehemiah. However effectively you may
be serving the Lord now, the study of Nehemiah will help you
serve Him better.

*My Father and my God, teach me more of what I really need
to know. In Jesus' Name. Amen.*

FIRST THINGS FIRST

FOR READING & MEDITATION – NEHEMIAH 1: 1–2

Hanani, one of my brothers, came from Judah with
some other men, and I questioned them … (v 2)

Nehemiah, a Jew, held a position of great eminence as cup-
bearer to the king of the Persian king. Nehemiah's brother,
Hanani, reports that the gates and walls of Jerusalem are broken
down because of the decline in spirituality and general apathy. In
addition marauders had burned down the gates and reduced them
to a pile of ashes. Jerusalem, the city of God, was in a sorry state.

Nehemiah's strong reaction to this news shows us where his
real concerns lay: not in maintaining a good position in the Persian Empire but in achieving God's purposes for his holy city.

What is our reaction when we observe, for example, the 'walls'
of the most precious institution of marriage and family life in
danger of being demolished? How do we react when we see God's
principles disregarded? Do our personal concerns take priority over
God's concerns? Nehemiah put first things first. So must we.

Rebuilding broken walls

JULY 2

*O God, give us the same spirit that Nehemiah had, who made
your priorities his priorities. In Christ's Name we pray. Amen.*

FACE IT AND FEEL IT

FOR READING & MEDITATION – NEHEMIAH 1:3

… Those who survived the exile and are back in
the province are in great trouble and disgrace. (v 3)

When Nehemiah heard that the walls of Jerusalem were still
in ruins and the city gates had been burned to the ground,
he sat down and wept.

A number of Christians think that because we are 'partakers of
the divine nature' we should never feel sad. Regardless of our spiritual maturity, we will feel the pain of misfortune or loss acutely.

The first thing to do when confronted by disaster or loss is to
face and feel it. To pretend that we do not is not evidence of maturity but of immaturity. We are not to wallow in these emotions but
we must be willing to feel them for *unacknowledged emotions
cause trouble.* Integrity requires that whatever is true must be faced
– troublesome emotions too. Nehemiah was no less godly because
he gave vent to his emotions. It's the healthy thing to do.

Rebuilding broken walls

JULY 3

O Father, help me see that facing and feeling the emotions
that arise within me is not a sign of faithlessness. Amen.

WEEPING OVER THE RUINS

FOR READING & MEDITATION – NEHEMIAH 1:3

The wall of Jerusalem is broken down,
and its gates have been burned with fire. (v 3)

Nehemiah wept over the condition of Jerusalem. Our Lord wept for the city too. We are fit to do God's work only when we accept the truth about a situation. Look around you today and see things as they are, not as you would like them to be. Are you aware of any broken-down 'walls'? The walls of your devotional life perhaps. Your family. Your church. Is there something for which you should be grieving at this moment? A ruin you are not prepared to acknowledge?.

Nehemiah's intensely emotional reaction to the news of Jerusalem highlights the first of the many spiritual principles we shall discover in following his story: *before anyone can receive a blessing someone else has to be willing to bear a burden.* We can never lighten the load for others until we have first felt the weight of their troubles in our own soul.

O God, help me discover if there are any ruins in my life and, if so, recognise them and grieve over them. In Jesus' Name. Amen.

ATTITUDE FIXES ALTITUDE

FOR READING & MEDITATION – NEHEMIAH 1:4–7

For some days I mourned and fasted and
prayed before the God of heaven. (v 4)

Walls cannot be rebuilt until we see the ruins in which they lie. When we have a vision of spiritual ruin we should do what Nehemiah did – turn to fervent believing prayer.

Nehemiah reminds the Almighty of his greatness and the fact that He is a covenant-keeping God. He stands in both awe and adoration before Him, recognising his sovereignty. *The greater God becomes to him, the smaller his problem appears in comparison.* Nehemiah is then moved to confess the sins of his people and admits that their troubles stemmed from disobedience.

The attitude underlying Nehemiah's prayer is important to note: it is an attitude of reverence and submission. One person has said, 'The self-sufficient do not pray; they merely talk to themselves. The self-satisfied will not pray; they have no knowledge of their need. The self-righteous cannot pray; they have no basis on which to come to God.' 'When there is no reverence for God there will be few answers from God.

🖝 *Father, teach me to pray, dear Lord, as You once taught your disciples. Amen.*

THE PROMISE-KEEPER

FOR READING & MEDITATION – NEHEMIAH 1:8–11

O LORD, let your ear be attentive to
the prayer of this your servant ... (v 11)

In claiming the provision God made for his people, the godly Nehemiah reveals another great principle: he claims the fulfilment of the promise. Nehemiah's confidence in the Lord as a Promise-Keeper is so great that he knows God will work out the details. Nehemiah knows it will be harder for him to leave the court than it was to enter it. He is a trusted and important man. But he accepts, too, that with God all things are possible.

God does not hear our prayers so much as hear *us* – in other words, what we put of ourselves into our prayers. Nehemiah continued entreating the Lord's favour for four months!

Do we hear Nehemiah's kind of praying nowadays? Sadly, not as often as we ought. Most modern-day prayers are token prayers asking God to bless this, that and the other. Powerful praying flows out of seeing the situation as it is. And in seeing God as He is.

My Father and my God, help me to fuse You and the need together in fervent believing prayer. Amen.

THE WAITING TEST

FOR READING & MEDITATION – NEHEMIAH 2:1–2

... the king asked me, 'Why does your face look
so sad when you are not ill?' (v 2)

We find Nehemiah still waiting for an answer to his prayer.
It has been four months now since he first heard the news
concerning Jerusalem, during which time he has wept, mourned,
fasted, and prayed.

As it happened Nehemiah did not have to speak to the king. Ar-
taxerxes invites Nehemiah to share the reason for his sadness. The
initiative is no longer in Nehemiah's hands; it is in God's.

How important is timing in all that we seek to do for God. Many
a life has been shipwrecked spiritually because of impulsiveness
and haste. I know people who could have been in a great ministry
today but they failed the waiting test. Some say the need is the
call, but God's timing must be sought in everything we do. A right
action can turn out to be wrong simply because it was mistimed.
God's timing is always perfect. Ours is not.

🐦 *O Father, show me even more clearly the need to adjust my
spiritual clock to Yours. In Jesus' Name. Amen.*

PRAYER-O-GRAMS

For reading & meditation – Nehemiah 2:3–5

Then I prayed to the God of heaven … (v 4)

Nehemiah's detailed request in response to the king's question concerning his sad countenance was not something that resulted from his prayer-o-gram. *That* was a quick request for help as he presented his petition to visit Jerusalem in order to help his people. You can be sure that the details of that petition had been worked out in hours of prolonged intercession over a period of four months. How persistently and passionately he must have pleaded with God concerning his position at the court.

How different things might be if we could learn to bend the knee in supplication whenever we face a difficult or delicate situation.

Prayer-o-grams have their place, but they must never be seen as substitutes for fervent, believing intercession. We would all like to be able to pray Ford prayers and get Rolls-Royce blessings. But some rewards in prayer come only in proportion to the effort.

Father, I see there is a place for prayer-o-grams and a place for persistent intercession. Help me understand the purpose of both and utilise both. In Jesus' Name I pray. Amen.

SAFE, SENT AND SUPPLIED

FOR READING & MEDITATION – NEHEMIAH 2:6–9
And because the gracious hand of my God was upon me,
the king granted my requests. (v 8)

Just how profitable the four months were that Nehemiah spent
fasting and praying can be seen from the well thought-out presentation he made to the king; a petition that covered his every need.

This ought to encourage us to be bold in our praying. As the
hymnist put it: 'We are coming to a King. Large petitions we must
bring.' Though Nehemiah had worked hard on his petition, he
does not take the credit when the king grants his requests, but sees
it as evidence of the gracious hand of the Lord upon him (v 8).

Nehemiah must have been greatly heartened before setting out
on his journey to know he had been sent by the king, had his
guarantee of a safe passage, and that all his needs would be supplied. Sent, safe, supplied – all these things are supremely important if we are to be successful in what we do for God.

*O Father, help me to have Nehemiah's dependent and humble
attitude. This I ask in our Lord's peerless Name. Amen.*

ARE WE KNOWN IN HELL?

FOR READING & MEDITATION – NEHEMIAH 2:10

When Sanballat ... and Tobiah ... heard about this,
they were very much disturbed ... (v 10)

Sanballat, the governor of Samaria, and Tobiah his associate knew Nehemiah was on his way to rebuild Jerusalem. They were men of influence and power who opposed and tried to out-manoeuvre Nehemiah in everything that he did. War was declared in the heavens; they would focus their hatred on the Lord but on his servant also. No battle can commence anywhere, in the spiritual sense, until somebody decides to stand up and challenge the things that need challenging.

How much overtime has the devil to put in, I wonder, because of our willingness to stand up and do something for God? Or to put it another way: How well are we known in hell? One thing is sure – when we stand up and are counted as citizens of the kingdom then Satan will throw all his weight against us. If you don't want a spiritual battle then stay seated.

Rebuilding broken walls

JULY 10

🕊 *O God, how can I stay seated when so much is at stake? Give me the courage to stand up and be counted. In Christ's Name. Amen.*

WHILE OTHERS SLEPT

FOR READING & MEDITATION – NEHEMIAH 1:11–16

I had not told anyone what my God had put
in my heart to do for Jerusalem. (v 12)

In Jerusalem Nehemiah sets out on horseback, presumably at night
so as not to alert Israel's enemies to his intentions too early.

We can only conjecture as to what Nehemiah felt that night as
he reconnoitred the city. Jerusalem had once been a mighty for-
tress with its walls standing tall and strong. Now it was in a sad
and sorry state. How he must have wept as he took in the distress-
ing picture.

Some Christians believe that we should not even look at anything negative in case it becomes an impediment to faith. What
kind of faith is it that can't be upheld while facing things as they
really are? We don't have to linger over negative situations, but we
do have to look at them. All great movements of God begin with
someone who, like Nehemiah, is brave enough to look fully at the
facts, analyse what should be done, then rise to the task.

Rebuilding broken walls

☙ *My Father and my God, help me understand how to be a realist without being a pessimist. Amen.*

'COME, LET US REBUILD'

For reading & meditation – Nehemiah 2:17–18

Come, let us rebuild the wall of Jerusalem,
and we will no longer be in disgrace. (v 17)

Once Nehemiah is in possession of the facts, he convenes a meeting of all the inhabitants, and in his address draws their attention to the need for a careful evaluation of their plight. 'You see the trouble we are in,' he says, 'Jerusalem lies in ruins ... Come, let us rebuild the wall.'

Are there 'walls' in your life lying flat that should be standing? Perhaps once you were on fire for God but now you rationalise your Christian experience and comment: 'Life nowadays is tough.' Dangerous thinking.

Take a look around. See the walls that are lying flat? That is not what God wants. Ruined walls do not glorify God. *Come, let us rebuild.* I am discovering some 'walls' in my own life that need rebuilding. I wonder, is it the same with you? If so, let's begin re-building – and without delay.

O Father, I hear your call to rebuild – and I respond. I will take the first steps towards this today. Help me dear Father. In Jesus' Name. Amen.

'IN JESUS' NAME GET OUT'

For reading & meditation – Nehemiah 2:19–20

The God of heaven will give us success. (v 20)

When we hear the challenge 'Come, let us rebuild' Satan quickly marshals his forces and says, 'Come, let us destroy.'

Sanballat, Tobiah and Geshem the Arab (another powerful ruler) are at hand to oppose Nehemiah, knowing full well that weak, demoralised people are inclined to give way when threatened. But they reckon without Nehemiah! Before the Jews have time to re-act, Nehemiah makes his reply: ' The God of heaven will give us success,' he says. 'We his servants will start rebuilding.'

How desperately we need men and women like this in the Church today; people who will stand up to the devil and say: 'Make all the threats you like. We will not be diverted from our purpose of building walls in God's kingdom and bringing praise and glory to our King. It's time to say to him: 'In the Name of Jesus get out.'

O Father, forgive us for our timidity when facing Satan and his forces. Help us rise up and give him his marching orders. For your own dear Name's sake. Amen.

FIRST PRINCIPLES

FOR READING & MEDITATION – NEHEMIAH 3:1–2

Eliashib the high priest and his fellow priests
went to work and rebuilt the Sheep Gate. (v 1)

Under Nehemiah's inspiring leadership, the first to get going
are the priests.

It must have been an amazing sight to see Eliashib the High
Priest and all the other priests giving themselves enthusiastically to
the rebuilding of the wall. Management experts tell us one of the
first principles of leadership is *co-ordination*. This involves blend-
ing people and their activities together in a way that successfully
contributes to the whole, a principle much at work in this chapter.

While the Church should not think of itself as a business affair,
it ought nevertheless to be businesslike in all its affairs. Co-ordination is needed as greatly in the Church as it is in business. Those
churches with the pastor-does-it-all approach will never develop
properly. Such an attitude curbs the ministry which God has given
to *every* believer. No co-ordination – no corporate or individual
development and growth. It is as simple as that.

☞ *Father, raise up many more modern-day Nehemiahs to help
co-ordinate the abilities that in many parts of your Church lie un-
developed. In Jesus' Name. Amen.*

THE UNBENDING NECK

FOR READING & MEDITATION – NEHEMIAH 3:3–5

... but their nobles would not put their shoulders
to the work under their supervisors. (v 5)

First we see the sons of Hassenaah at work rebuilding the Fish
Gate. This was one of Jerusalem's key gates, and doubtless the
workers gave themselves to the task of reconstruction with energy, enthusiasm and skill. However, there is one jarring note in
these verses: 'The next section was repaired by the men of Tekoa,
but their nobles would not put their shoulders to the work under
their supervisors.'

Their problem, I think, was not so much lethargy as pride. The
word translated 'shoulders' in the text means 'back of the neck'
and is taken from the imagery of oxen refusing to yield to the yoke.
The unbending neck is a standard picture of pride in the Bible.

Pride, we must not forget, was the very first sin. It turned an
angel into the devil. There will never be much spiritual progress
where there is pride. Keep this always in mind – pride must die in
us if Christ is to live in us.

Lord Jesus Christ, deliver me from the unbending neck and
an unbiddable attitude. Amen.

T·E·A·M·W·O·R·K

For reading & meditation – Nehemiah 3:6–7

... repairs were made by men from Gibeon and Mizpah ...
places under the ... governor of Trans-Euphrates. (v 7)

Another important principle of leadership is *co-operation*. This third chapter illustrates Nehemiah's ability to get people to work closely together. Under God he brings together a powerful taskforce from different walks of life – priests, Levites, rulers and common people, merchants, Temple servants, guards, farmers, goldsmiths.

I heard one management expert say the word *success* should be spelt 't-e-a-m-w-o-r-k'. His observation that 'if the whole prospers the individual will prosper' deserves emphasis. Men from Gibeon and Mizpah carried out repairs. They could easily have allowed their own interests to draw them away from such personally unrewarding work. Though they lived some distance from Jerusalem it was a matter of great concern to them that these symbols of God's glory should be restored.

If we belong to Christ then all personal preoccupations and interests ought to be secondary to the building up of his kingdom. Nothing, nothing must take precedence over this.

Father, I take this challenge to heart. Give me grace to make your priorities my priorities. In Christ's Name I pray. Amen.

SIDE BY SIDE

For reading & meditation – Nehemiah – 3:8–12

Shallum … repaired the next section
with the help of his daughters. (v 12)

It is clear that Nehemiah was skilful in getting men and women
from all walks of life to co-operate in the rebuilding of Jerusalem's walls.

The rulers laboured shoulder to shoulder with the others. In
one of the verses before us we see that one of the officials, a man
named Shallum, was being assisted by his daughters. These young
women showed they were not afraid to soil their hands with work
normally done by men.

How was Nehemiah able to get people from different walks of
life to co-operate with each other in this way? It was by his inspiring leadership and example. The godly Nehemiah was able to set
before them the vision of what ought to be done, then fire them
with the importance of that task.

How desperately we stand in need of such leadership in the
Church today.

🐦 *My Father and my God, help me to be part of the movement of
the Spirit that prays for the kind of leadership that both the Church
and the world stand in need of. Amen.*

EXPRESSING APPRECIATION

FOR READING & MEDITATION – NEHEMIAH 3:13–14
They also repaired five hundred yards
of the wall as far as the Dung Gate. (v 13)

Management experts consider *commendation* a third princi-ple of successful leadership. By this is meant a readiness to note and praise honest effort and to take a personal interest in those for whom one is responsible. Although we do not see Nehemiah actively going around praising people, we certainly see him taking a strong personal interest in his workers.

The recital of the names of all the people who worked on the different gates reveals a lot about Nehemiah's awareness of who each person was, what they did and where they worked. It comes across also in the oft-repeated word *repairs*. In Nehemiah's eyes every person had the same worth and was not to be manipulated or exploited.

Every one of us needs to feel that we count for something. God, of course, appreciates us. Scripture leaves us in no doubt about that. But it's nice to be appreciated by those with skin on also.

O God, forgive me if, when I feel unappreciated, I use that fact as an excuse for not expressing appreciation to others. Amen.

'GOOD WORK, MALKIJAH'

The Dung Gate was repaired by Malkijah ... ruler
of the district of Beth Hakkerem. (v 14)

The term commendation is not actually mentioned, but the
principle can be discovered nevertheless. Nehemiah was aware
of the position of each of his workers and knew them all by name.
He must have shown that same kind of concern in his personal
relationships with them day by day. 'Good work, Malkijah,' I can
hear him say.

We live in an age of depersonalisation. Often we are identified
by numbers rather than names. Some psychologists conducted an
experiment on a group of volunteers who were isolated for a
month and referred to by number rather than by name. At the
end of the month's experiment each member of the group experienced depression to a varying degree, and all appeared to suffer
from a temporary loss of self-worth.

Mark Twain commented that he could live for a whole month
on a compliment. It's sad that we are far more ready to criticise
than commend.

*O Father, save me from looking for matters to criticise rather
than those I can commend. In Christ's Name. Amen.*

HOUSE REPAIRS!

For reading & meditation – Nehemiah 3:28–32

Above the Horse Gate, the priests made repairs,
each in front of his own house. (v 28)

Nehemiah arranged for each worker to build near his own home. This served two purposes: first, it relieved the men of unnecessary anxiety in the event of an attack (they would want to be close to their families), and second, it gave them a deep sense of family closeness as they were building.

Nehemiah knew that the home was of prime importance. This is where every real work of God must begin and be anchored. One of the alarming trends in today's society is the rapid disappearance of homes where Christ rules and where Biblical principles prevail. Such homes are becoming hard to find.

What are the spiritual walls like around your home? The walls of prayer, the family altar, integrity, faithfulness, openness, and so on? Commit yourself to undertaking any spiritual repairs that may be needed in your house. And let Christ be the Head of your home.

O Father, Help me rebuild any walls that may be broken down in my family life, beginning with my own personal commitment and dedication to You. Amen.

A LEADER'S KNACK

FOR READING & MEDITATION – NEEKIAH 3:28–32
... between the room above the corner and the Sheep Gate
the goldsmiths and merchants made repairs. (v 32)

Long before 'management seminars' were in vogue Nehemiah
employed the principles which today's experts claim are essential if one is to be a good and inspiring leader. He co-ordinated the
efforts of the workers, inspired their co-operation by setting before them a clear vision, and commended them for their sacrificial
efforts. The fourth in the list of good management principles is:
communication. This involves the instruction of each worker so
that he or she knows what to do and where to do it, and the del-
egation of authority so that decisions do not need to be constantly
referred to the top.

The principles of leadership may be applied to whatever the Lord
has called us to do. I am praying that many reading these lines may
learn from Nehemiah how to lay down their own foundation for
leadership.

🐾 *Father, I see that things work according to certain principles;*
they don't just happen. Teach me the principles governing spiritual
success and help me keep to them – no matter what. In Christ's
Name. Amen.

UNBEATABLE AND UNBREAKABLE

Can they bring the stones back to life from those
heaps of rubble – burned as they are?' (v 2)

Whenever a work for God gets under way it is not long before
Satan begins to stir up opposition.

Sarcasm, derision and invective are some of Satan's chief weapons when attempting to discourage God's people. I have known continued sarcasm to cause men to leave the Christian ministry and return to secular employment.

I wonder how many of you, as you go about your secular tasks, will receive some carping remark about your faith from your colleagues. Or perhaps from your own family. Satan can use even our loved ones to discourage us. Some Christians think God should preserve us from such discouragement. However, his way is not to save us from it, but to save us in it. Only when we learn to accept this fact will we be unbeatable and unbreakable.

Rebuilding broken walls

JULY 22

Father, my soul shrinks from criticism and sarcasm but teach me how to absorb the grace that makes me more than a match for even that. In Jesus' Name. Amen.

WHAT A PRAYER!

For reading & meditation – Nehemiah 4:4–5

Do not cover up their guilt or blot out
their sins from your sight … (v 5)

When Nehemiah was faced with criticism, he poured out his
heart to God in prayer. And what a prayer it is! The nature
of his prayer has been a source of embarrassment to Christians
down the ages considering what the New Testament teaches concerning loving one's enemies. Why did God allow a prayer of this
nature to be recorded?

My old tutor at the college I attended said: 'You have to be a
very spiritual person to pray that kind of prayer.' His reply made
me think deeply: Nehemiah did not take action against those who
opposed him but invited God to redress the wrong. Many of us
when opposed might feel like praying in this fashion but usually
our prayer is prompted more by a grudge at what is happening to
us than grief at what is happening to the work of God.

Rebuilding broken walls

✽ *O Father, much of my praying is governed more by a grudge
towards others than grief at what is happening to your honour.
Help me stop such praying. Amen.*

FAITH VERSUS FEAR

FOR READING & MEDITATION – NEHEMIAH 4:6–11

... for the people worked with all their heart. (v 6)

On hearing further reports about the success of Nehemiah's mission the enemies of Judah decide to wage war against Jerusalem.

Nehemiah turns once more to prayer. But this time the situation demands not only prayer but action. 'But we prayed to our God,' he says, '*and* posted a guard' (v 9).

There are times when prayer is enough to deal with a situation, but there are other times when prayer needs to be accompanied by action. Faith must join hands with works.

Some of the people in Judah became discouraged and wanted to quit. Nehemiah knew the reason was fear. This is why he turned their attention to the Lord who is 'great and awesome' (v 14).

Fear can only be overcome with faith; not faith in oneself but faith in God. Is fear knocking at your door right now? Then, as you answer its knock, take Jesus with you. Don't be surprised if you find no one there.

Lord Jesus Christ, You had a heart that was unafraid. Give that same heart to me even now. For your own dear Name's sake. Amen.

ARMED FOR WARFARE

For reading & meditation – Nehemiah 4:12–20
Our God will fight for us! (v 20)

Nehemiah's three-pronged counter-attack – prayer, vigilant guards and the charge to look continually to the Lord – is so successful that he is able to write: 'We all returned to the wall, each to his own work' (v 15).

As we seek to rebuild the walls that have been broken down either by neglect or by Satan and his forces, let us not forget that we are engaged in a battle as well as in a building programme. We must go about our task with a sword in one hand and a trowel in the other.

In addition to the gifts God has given us to build his kingdom in this world, we need a sword to defend ourselves against Satan and his forces. The sword of the Spirit is the Word of God, and the more we memorise the Word and meditate on it, the stronger will be our resistance to the devil and his armies.

O God, help me not to become so taken up with aspects of spiritual warfare that I lose sight of the essential building work. Amen.

DON'T GET IN A RUT!

FOR READING & MEDITATION – NEHEMIAH 4:21–23

So we continued the work with half the men
holding spears, from the first light of dawn. (v 21)

The final verses of this chapter show us better than any others the chief reason for Nehemiah's success. *He was one with the people.* He was willing to endure the same privations, suffer the same hardships and face the same dangers as everyone else.

Leaders today could learn a lot from studying how Nehemiah handled himself during these trying times. When a difficult situation arose he faced it objectively and confidently, believing that nothing could ever overtake him that God and he could not work out together.

To reorder our priorities is something we all ought to be open to, whether or not we are leaders. Those who are not willing to do this get stuck in a rut. When you're in a rut be careful for it has been said, 'The only difference between a rut and a grave is its depth.'

🐚 *O God, whatever reviews are necessary in my life, help me to rise to them in the strength that comes from You. Amen.*

RICH MAN – POOR MAN

FOR READING & MEDITATION – NEHEMIAH 5:1–5

Now the men and their wives raised a great outcry
against their Jewish brothers. (v 1)

The rebuilding of Jerusalem's walls now take second place to a
more pressing problem – internal dissension, because of a
food crisis, the effects of which were made worse by the increased
number of Jews in Jerusalem. Some rich Jews were feathering
their nests and generally exploiting those who were in financial
difficulty.

The most difficult tensions to resolve in society are those which
exist between the rich and the poor, the affluent and the under-
privileged. James wrote of this problem in his epistle (see James 2:
1–13), and it continues to plague society to this very day. God had
decreed that to make provision for the poor, the rich were to lend
to them (Deut 15:7–11) without charging interest (Ex 22:25; Lev
25:36). But these wise provisions had become a dead letter.

When we disregard any of God's rules for living as laid down in
Scripture we expose ourselves to troubles. We take his way or we
take the consequences. Period.

*O God, help me take your way in everything, dear Lord. In
Jesus' Name. Amen.*

WHEN VERY ANGRY

FOR READING & MEDITATION – NEHEMIAH 5:6

When I heard their outcry and these charges, I was very angry. (v 6)

Faced with this new problem of internal dissension, how does Nehemiah react? He becomes very angry.

Watch how Nehemiah handles his anger. First he acknowledges them (v 6). He does not excuse his feelings or minimise them. He admits that he had been very angry. And he doesn't dump his feelings on others either. He keeps his anger under control.

Then he takes time to ponder and evaluate the situation (v 7). By carefully weighing all the issues and thinking matters through, he is able to find the right strategy for dealing with the situation.

How different our lives would be if, whenever we became angry, we followed Nehemiah's example. First, acknowledge the anger. Second, choose not to allow it to get out of control. Third, carefully and prayerfully think through the best way of dealing with the situation which aroused the anger in the first place. Easier said than done? Maybe. Why don't you try it and see.

Rebuilding broken walls

JULY 28

My Father and my God, help me follow these principles the next time I feel anger rise within me. Amen.

DOING WHAT IS RIGHT

For reading & meditation – Nehemiah 5:7–11

... 'What you are doing is not right.' (v 9)

Nehemiah knew what was being practised by the loan sharks, so he courageously confronts the hierarchy of Jerusalem privately, then calls a large meeting. He spells out his objections and challenges the nobles to return to the Lord. He reproaches the leaders and goes on to say that the people they sold to the Gentiles have been bought back by Nehemiah and his friends. Nehemiah reproves them for not walking 'in the fear of our God', and challenges them to return the land, property and interest.

Sometimes more is needed than just to think through issues objectively; we need courage also to face and confront those with whom we strongly disagree. Many of us are content to settle for being right. Only under extreme provocation do we discuss the cause of our anger or concern with the offending party. It is all too easy to find reasons for not doing what we know needs to be done.

My Father, help me not to be complacent about issues that need to be confronted. Amen.

WALKING HIS WAY

FOR READING & MEDITATION – NEHEMIAH 5:7–11

Shouldn't you walk in the fear of our God ... (v 9)

Yesterday we watched Nehemiah deal with his anger in a positive and productive way. Now we watch him as he puts into action the ideas that came to him as he carefully thought through the situation, so Nehemiah courageously confronts those in the wrong.

Over the years I have observed that people handle anger in several different ways. Some get angry but convince themselves they are not. These people live in denial. Though they may not realise it, unacknowledged anger finds a way to leak out – sometimes into the physical system in the form of muscular or other physiological problems. Others feel anger and proceed to deal with it by dumping it on everyone in sight. Then there are some who experience anger but suppress it for a while and later take their feelings out on those they know are afraid of them.

Rebuilding broken walls

My Father and my God, strengthen my resolve to deal with things that need dealing with not merely because I am provoked but because it is right to do so. In Jesus' Name. Amen.

HOW A DAY SHOULD END

For reading & meditation – Nehemiah 5:12–13

… the whole assembly said, 'Amen,' and praised the Lord. (v 13)

Under Nehemiah's strong rebuke the wealthy money-lenders promise to give up their extortionate practices. Nehemiah knows human nature too well, and thus he demands an oath.

Nehemiah was a wise leader and realist and would not leave anything to chance. He asks the leaders for a formal commitment, and validates their promise by a symbolic act. He shakes out the folds of his robe as a sign that God will reject the people if they fail to keep their promise.

As this is done the whole assembly responds with a loud 'Amen'. In this instance, however, not only did the people say 'Amen', but they broke out in a spontaneous act of worship and praise. Thus a day that began in sorrow ends in spiritual rejoicing. But then, when wrongs are righted and God's Word honoured, it always does.

O God our Father, help me never to come to the end of a day without righting all wrongs, forgiving all trespasses and ensuring that my life is in line with your Word. Amen.

JULY 31 | *Rebuilding broken walls*

THE FEAR OF THE LORD

FOR READING & MEDITATION – NEHEMIAH 5:14–15
'But out of reverence for God I did not act like that.' (v 15)

In the words before us we discover the dynamic that motivated the godly Nehemiah – *reverence for God*. Reverence for the Lord is described in Scripture as the foundation of right conduct (Ps 111:10; Prov 1:7). Underlying 'reverence for God' or 'the fear of the Lord', is *holiness*. No one can ascend the hill of the Lord, we are told in the Psalms, unless he has clean hands and a pure heart (Ps 24:3–4). And 'without holiness no-one will see the Lord' (Heb 12:14).

In an age when standards are being lowered and moral absolutes ignored, it is so easy to rationalise issues and cut corners morally on the basis that everyone else is doing the same. But blessed are those who, like Nehemiah, stand up for truth and righteousness and say, 'But out of reverence for God I did not act like that.'

O God, give me today a fresh vision of what it means to revere You. And may that reverence show itself in all I do and say. For Jesus' sake. Amen.

SAYING 'YES'

FOR READING & MEDITATION – NEHEMIAH 5:16–19

Remember me with favour, O my God, for all
I have done for these people. (v 19)

From Nehemiah's example another important principle emerges – *single-mindedness*. Nehemiah's decision to devote himself to rebuilding the wall instead of developing an affluent lifestyle shows him to have been purposeful and committed to one task. He did not get caught up with private ventures or peripheral issues with their distractions. Instead he concentrated on one thing only.

Whatever we are called to do for God, we will not experience success unless we are single-minded. More is required of us as Christians than turning our backs on that which is negative; we must also turn our faces towards the positive, the will and purpose of God.

The secret of success in the Christian life is not just saying 'No' to whatever is wrong, but saying 'Yes' to what is right.

Nehemiah's prayer, with which this chapter closes, provides us with one more insight into his *modus operandi*. He did nothing important without lifting his heart to God in prayer. Neither should we.

Gracious and loving Father, give me a prayerful heart. In Jesus' Name. Amen.

A TRAP OF THE DEVIL

FOR READING & MEDITATION – NEHEMIAH 6:1–4

I am carrying on a great project and cannot go down. (v 3)

When Sanballat, Tobiah and Geshem receive the news that Jerusalem's walls have been rebuilt they are incensed and decide to attack Nehemiah personally. Even though they sent the same message four times, his answer remained: 'I am carrying on a great project.' Nehemiah's place was in Jerusalem, and nothing would draw him away.

There are times when the temptation that came to Nehemiah comes also to those seeking to do something special for God. It is the temptation to give up what we are doing in the interests of tact and diplomacy. The devil steps up to us and whispers, 'Stop what you are doing and explain your actions to others. Diplomacy and dialogue will help you get your work done faster.' There may be a place for diplomacy and dialogue, but the situation must be evaluated most carefully. Sometimes the suggestion can be a trap of the devil – calculated to divert you from your God-given task.

O God, may I be willing to listen to others but always obedient to You. In Christ's Name. Amen.

QUIET CONFIDENCE

For reading & meditation – Nehemiah 6:5–9

But I prayed, ' Now strengthen my hands.' (v 9)

Sanballat now tries a new approach – *innuendo*. He sends an open letter with the implication of treason. He is aware that this letter will be made known to the public and may well blacken Nehemiah's character and undermine his influence.

This attack on Nehemiah exploited a well-known quirk in the human personality, namely the willingness to believe the worst about others. Think how quickly scandal runs through an office, an organisation or even a church. With the faintest hint of indiscreet behaviour the person concerned is soon labelled 'guilty'. Nehemiah rebuts the attack with a definite denial and once again turns to prayer.

The godly Nehemiah prayed that his hands might be strengthened so that the work might prosper. He was happy to leave his reputation and future to the One he served. That's quiet confidence – the kind, if we know Nehemiah's God, we can have too.

Gracious and loving heavenly Father, help me to know You in the way that Nehemiah knew You so that I may have that same confidence too. In Jesus' Name I pray. Amen.

OUTWITTED, OUTMANOEUVRED

For reading & meditation – Nehemiah 6:10–14

Remember Tobiah and Sanballat, O my God,

because of what they have done ... (v 14)

Nehemiah visits the house of Shemaiah as the final stage of the building programme is being completed. Shemaiah tries to convince Nehemiah that his life is in danger and that they must both flee to the Temple.

Nehemiah's reply is blunt: 'Should a man like me run away? Or should one like me go into the temple to save his life?' (v 11). If Nehemiah had gone with Shemaiah into the Holy Place he would have laid himself open to two charges: one, cowardice, and the other, violation of the law that permitted only priests to stand in that Holy Place.

Nehemiah's encounter with Shemaiah leaves him with a deep sense of his vulnerability, and so once again his heart turns to the Lord in prayer. Nehemiah's life and reputation have been preserved not by breaking God's laws but by keeping them. When we do what is right, we can leave all the consequences with God. Take it to heart and be encouraged.

O Father, You are able to outmanoeuvre everybody and everything. My heart rejoices in You. Amen.

THE IMPORTANCE OF PRAYER

FOR READING & MEDITATION – NEHEMIAH 6:15–19

So the wall was completed on the twenty-fifth
of Elul, in fifty-two days. (v 15)

The whole job of rebuilding the wall took just fifty-two days.
When those who had opposed Nehemiah's work hear of his
success they lose some of their self-confidence because they realise
that such a project could never have been accomplished without
the help of the Almighty.

The last few sentences of this chapter lead us once again to see
what a spiritual stalwart Nehemiah was. Despite all the pressures,
despite enemies who were still plotting, he maintained his confidence in God. A man of lesser ability and character would have
given up. It has been said, 'A man has no more character than is
revealed when he is in a crisis.' We must never forget that the
foundation of spiritual success is our personal character. Whatever
else we may have, if we don't have character it amounts to little
or nothing.

*Gracious Father, so that I am ready for the moment of crisis,
deposit within me the lineaments of your own character. May the
beauty of Jesus be seen in me. Amen.*

GAINS MUST BE GUARDED

FOR READING & MEDITATION – NEHEMIAH 7:1–3

… Hananiah … was a man of integrity and
feared God more than most men do. (v 2)

The first six chapters deal with the reconstruction of Jerusalem's
walls. As Nehemiah initiates 'Phase Two' – the re-instruction of
the people – he creates his own brother Hanani governor of Jerusalem, for in Hanani he saw a man who was concerned for others.

Hananiah, a man of integrity, who feared God more than most
men do, is appointed to be commander of the citadel. These men
were sorely needed with traitorous Jews in high places and leading families involved in intrigue. Then, having ensured that certain residents will act as watchmen, Nehemiah gives Hanani and
Hananiah instructions on how to safeguard the city.

It is always a mistake to think that because spiritual objectives
have been reached nothing more needs to be done. Gains must be
guarded. Times of great spiritual achievement can be as dangerous as times of disappointment if they put us off our guard. Vigi-
lance is required of us at all times.

*My Lord and my God, help me to be always vigilant. In Jesus'
Name I pray. Amen.*

TAKING STOCK OF THE PAST

So my God put it into my heart to assemble
[the people] for registration by families. (v 5)

Nehemiah is prompted by the Lord to register the people. Yet again we see how close a relationship this man had with the Lord. Note the words: 'So my God put it into my heart.'

The purpose of the census is to determine the genealogical purity of the people and of the priesthood in anticipation of the repopulation of the city. Chapter 7 is transitional and records the first step towards the consolidation of the work.

Before the people can enter into all that God has for them they must be sure of their inheritance and their calling. The same is true of us also. We need to know exactly what we have inherited in Christ if we are to enter into it. And what have we inherited? Life, peace, power, joy – riches beyond compare. It is one thing, however, to know of our inheritance. It is another to enter into it.

My Father, help me not merely to acknowledge my inheritance but appropriate it. In Jesus' Name. Amen.

PURITY IN THE PULPIT

FOR READING & MEDITATION – NEHEMIAH 7:39–69

… they could not find [their family records] and so
were excluded from the priesthood as unclean. (v 64)

In the section before us, we see listed a group of people who were
unable to show that their families had descended from Israel,
and among whom were a company of priests. These priests, because they could not prove their spiritual pedigree, were summar-
ily dismissed from the priesthood.

This might seem an extreme measure, especially as they had
had gained great experience in the ministry. But there is no room
for sentiment when it comes to God's instructions. A pure and
proper priesthood was essential if the people were to maintain a
right relationship with the Lord.

How I wish some leaders being ordained into the ministry nowadays were as faithful to the Word of God as was Nehemiah and
exclude from the pulpit those who have no clear spiritual testimo-
ny. Only those who have experienced the saving grace of Christ
can hope to minister that grace to others.

Rebuilding broken walls

🕊 *O God my Father, give us men like Nehemiah who will help
preserve our spiritual purity. In Christ's Name I pray. Amen.*

NO SACRIFICE – NO HOPE

FOR READING & MEDITATION – NEHEMIAH 7:70–73

Some of the heads of the families contributed to the work. (v 70)

Following the exclusion of the priests a spirit of liberality seemed to break out. Heading the list of people who willingly gave to the Lord's work were 'some of the heads of the families'. Their generous giving set an example which others quickly followed.

How wonderful it is when God's people take seriously the work of the ministry and give sacrificially for its support. I know churches whose ministers have had to take secular employment in order to support themselves. Such situations are a blot on the reputation of the Church and on the Name of our Lord Jesus Christ. Generosity generates generosity, and when people open their purse strings and give liberally to God's work great things happen.

One of the precursors to spiritual blessing in a church is the congregation's desire to show respect for the work of the ministry. Where there is no sacrifice in a congregation there is no hope for a congregation.

Our Father, it is your purpose that we be set not only in natural families but in spiritual families also. Amen.

HUNGRY FOR THE WORD!

For reading & meditation – Nehemiah 8:1–4

And all the people listened attentively to the Book of the Law. (v 3)

So universal is the spiritual awakening that the people leave their towns and make their way to Jerusalem 'as one man' to hear Ezra, the scribe, read the Scriptures to them.

The scribe, accompanied by thirteen priests, ascends the wooden platform built specially for this purpose and begins to read from the Word. The reading and explanation took five or six hours (this was no twenty-minute sermon!), during which time everyone listened attentively. As a consequence of such eagerness to listen to the Word of God something significant was bound to happen. And as we shall see a little later – it did.

Wouldn't it be wonderful if we had congregations eager enough to want to listen to the Word of God being expounded for five or six hours! When those who love to expound the Word and those who love hearing the Word expounded meet, anything can happen.

O God, forgive us if our souls are easily satisfied and we have lost the hunger to hear and understand your Word. Amen.

BACK TO THE BIBLE!

FOR READING & MEDITATION – NEHEMIAH 8:5–8

They read from the Book of the Law of God,
making it clear and giving the meaning. (v 8)

zra's reading and exposition of the Scriptures lasted five or six
hours. The point we need to get hold of from our passage is
this: it is not enough to hear the Word of God; it must also be
carefully explained. That is why God has gifted certain people in
the Church to explain the Scriptures.

When the great nineteenth-century Baptist preacher CH Spurgeon first came to London he noticed that the people who attended his church were so starved spiritually that even a morsel
of Biblical exposition was a treat to them. By the time he completed his ministry it was said that his people knew more of the
Bible than many a theologian.

Today churches tend to emphasise experience rather than Bible
exposition. People languish where the Word of God is not explained.

O God, help us as your people to put the Bible back in its proper
place. Raise up strong teachers to teach us and challenge us. For
your own dear Name's sake. Amen.

DON'T MOURN TOO LONG

For reading & meditation – Nehemiah 8:9–12

Do not grieve, for the joy of the LORD is your strength. (v 10)

Clearly the reading and exposition of God's Word has a profound effect upon the people, and they wept.

Nehemiah, Ezra and the Levites encourage the people to spend the rest of the day feasting and sharing their food with those who have nothing prepared. This instruction moves them from being too introspective and self-centred to being outgoing and other-centred. Other-centredness is always a good sign that God is at work in our hearts.

Nehemiah then reminds the people that the joy of the Lord is their strength. This statement puts the whole matter into perspective. Weeping and mourning ought to bring us to the end of our own resources so that we might discover our strength in the Lord. And what greater strength is there than in joy? And what greater joy is there than the joy of sins forgiven? We can live for God's glory only when we live in this kind of joy.

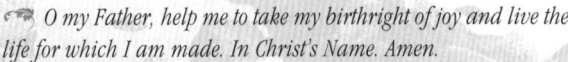

O my Father, help me to take my birthright of joy and live the life for which I am made. In Christ's Name. Amen.

INTO THE WORD – DAILY

For reading & meditation – Nehemiah 8:13–18
... the heads of all the families ... gathered around Ezra
... to give attention to the words of the Law. (v)13

Today we see how the spiritual movement that began in the five- or six-hour meeting culminates in the people desiring to know and do the will of the Lord.

As Ezra reads to them, they find they have not kept the Feast of Tabernacles which should take place during the seventh month. Once the heads of the families realise their oversight, they determine to remedy the situation at once. Their decision to keep the feast reveals their willingness to submit to the Word of God and do as it commands – not just to hear it.

So great is their longing to know more of God's Word that Ezra is asked to hold *daily* Bible studies. One day of teaching is not enough for these people – they want instruction on a regular basis. With such spiritual hunger, is it any wonder revival is in the air?

🕊 *Father, I do not simply want to feel good; I want to be good to obey You in all I do. Help me ever to do this. In Christ's Name. Amen.*

WHAT GALVANISES?

For reading & meditation – Nehemiah 9:1–5

They stood in their places and confessed their sins
and the wickedness of their fathers. (v 2)

Now we see the happy people going without food, dressed in sackcloth and with dust on their heads.

For three hours they stand confessing their sins and listening to the Word of God, and for a further three hours they worship the Lord. After this preparation the people are ready to be led in prayer. From their kneeling position they 'stand up and praise the Lord'.

Gone is all sense of inferiority and fear. Numerically they were weaker than their enemies, but their faith has been quickened.

A vastly different atmosphere would pervade our churches if only we would give more time to focusing our eyes on the Lord, listening to his Word being expounded and talking to Him in prayer. Nothing galvanises the human spirit and rids it of negativism and inferiority more effectively than time spent in the presence of the Eternal One.

O Father, I see that to become more like You I must spend more time with You. Help us to do that both individually and corporately. In Jesus' Name.

THE GOD-FOCUS

FOR READING & MEDITATION – NEHEMIAH 9:5–15

Blessed be your glorious name, and may it be exalted. (v 5)

This prayer, as we can see at once, is a prayer that is grounded in Scripture. If we are to pray powerfully and deeply then our minds must be soaked in Scripture. This seems to be a lost art nowadays. People in London said they gained as much from the prayers of Dr Martyn Lloyd-Jones as they did from his sermons. 'He prayed,' it was said, 'not only out of his heart but out of the Bible.' The more our prayers are rooted in the Bible, soaked in the Bible and in harmony with the Bible, the more powerful will be our praying.

Note how many times the word *You* appears in this section of the prayer. Clearly it is shot through with a God-focus. All great praying begins by focusing on God before focusing on anything else. When He is put in his rightful place then suddenly all other things appear in their rightful place. Try it and see.

O God, help me become more concerned with giving You glory than with getting something out of You. In Jesus' Name. Amen.

WHERE SIN ABOUNDS

FOR READING & MEDITATION – NEHEMIAH 9:16–25

They ate to the full and were well-nourished;
they revelled in your great goodness. (v 25)

In this section the word 'they' becomes prominent to remind the Israelites of their forefathers' stubbornness and sinfulness.

But the main focus of this part of the prayer is not on the sinfulness of the people but the marvellous mercy and forgiving grace of God. Where sin abounds, grace superabounds. Though Israel rebelled and chose to return to slavery in Egypt, the Lord stood by his people. Even when they made a golden calf and worshipped it He did not desert them (v 18), but continued to guide and protect them and provide everything they needed. Look at the way in which the words *You* and *they* are set against each other in describing the faithfulness of God and the stubbornness and recalcitrance of the people. God is faithful; the people unfaithful. God is consistent; the people are inconsistent. God is reliable; the people unreliable. How wonderful that God does not abandon us.

O God, how sad that we take your grace for granted. Forgive us and help us, dear Lord. In Jesus' Name. Amen.

DEVOUT REALISTS

FOR READING & MEDITATION – NEHEMIAH 9:26–31

But in your great mercy you did not put
an end to them or abandon them. (v 31)

This review of their national history provides every one of the
Jews listening with encouraging evidences of what God has
done in the past, the awesome consequences of ingratitude and the
inevitability of punishment if sin goes unconfessed. But most important
of all, there is hope for the future. And that hope is based
on the unchanging character of God. They see in the present a
product of the past and the seed of the future. Their anticipation
now is that the knowledge of past events will help them avoid the
evil and follow the good, which is Paul's message in 1 Corinthians
10:6 and 11.

A Biblical approach to history makes us neither wide-eyed optimists
nor downhearted pessimists. We become devout realists, for
we see God at work in all things and triumphing over everything.

*O God, help me build into my life times for reflection. In Jesus'
Name. Amen.*

'I WAS WRONG'

... you have acted faithfully, while we did wrong. (v 33)

One thing that strikes me about this whole prayer is the absence of excuses. True repentance always involves an admission of wrongdoing – without excuses. If we try to excuse ourselves by admitting, 'Lord, I know I was wrong in doing this, but I was a little unbalanced at the time because of all the pressures on me,' we are not truly repenting. Repentance offers no excuses, indulges in no prevarications or rationalisations.

We live in a day when people are quick to excuse themselves for their unacceptable behaviour by pleading, 'It's my parents' fault because they gave me a negative self-image. You can't blame me for the way I act.' Whatever you do, don't adopt this attitude when you come to God. Every one of us is culpable before Him. So let there be no excuses when we seek forgiveness from Him. Say those three little words – *I was wrong* – and cleansing will come hard on the heels of your confession.

O God, help me to take this truth – that confession of sin must contain no excuses for sin – and apply it to my life. Amen.

MAKING A COMMITMENT

FOR READING & MEDITATION – NEHEMIAH 9:32; 10:1–27
Those who sealed it were: Nehemiah the governor. (10:1)

Making a binding agreement to a deeper relationship with God is something every one of us ought to put into operation.

As a result of the exposition of Scripture and the powerful prayer of confession, the people decided to conserve the spiritual gains by entering into an agreement with God. The covenant was now signed and sealed by them.

First to set his seal to it was Nehemiah, next Zedekiah and the other priests, the Levites and representatives of all the people.

The scene must have been one of the most moving ever witnessed in the history of Israel as the leading people stood in line to sign and seal the covenant that committed them to keeping the commandments of the Lord. This kind of commitment arises from one thing only – the clear and anointed exposition of the Scriptures. Great things happen under the competent preaching of God's Word.

Father, I see that I too in times of spiritual crisis need to make a deep and dedicated commitment. Amen.

'MOST' IS NOT ENOUGH

For reading & meditation – Nehemiah 10:28–31

... all these now ... bind themselves with a curse
and an oath to follow the Law of God ... (v 29)

Nehemiah now focuses on the covenant itself. Their first commitment is the commitment to uphold all that is in God's Word.

From this general commitment the people go on to make more specific ones. First, they agree to abstain from intermarriage, a problem in Israel's history. Now they recognise that marriage to those who do not hold sacred things important creates great difficulties in a home. Spiritual differences result in the children being improperly instructed in the ways of the Lord, and this in turn undermines society. Next they commit themselves to keeping the Sabbath, and every seventh year allowing the ground to lie fallow and cancelling all debts.

Note the detail in this covenant. Not one matter is left unidentified. Remember that we must commit ourselves to obeying all the commandments of the Lord. 'Some' or 'most' is not enough.

O God, help me understand that through your Spirit You empower me to reach up to all your commandments. I am so deeply thankful. Amen.

WORSHIP IS CENTRAL

FOR READING & MEDITATION – NEHEMIAH 10:32–39
We will not neglect the house of our God. (v 39)

The people are agreeing that the Lord's claim on their lives will touch everything they have and own – children, cattle, produce, even the new wine and oil. Whether Ezra drafted the covenant on his own or with the help of others we cannot be sure, but clearly great care was taken to cover every area of their lives.

There is always a strong link between spirituality and social conduct, therefore the things which had to do with the Temple were not to be neglected. Unless the worship of God (represented by the house of God) is central, all kinds of social problems will arise. Without a strong base for worship neither the Church nor society can expect to survive.

Israel's covenant with the Lord contains important principles for the Church here in the twentieth century. Let us yield to his will and allow Him to develop within us a love for his Word, a deep desire to do his work, and a genuine concern to minister to those who, in Christ's Name, minister to us.

O God, how wonderful it would be if today all your people everywhere committed themselves to following You and serving You wholeheartedly. Amen.

URBAN RENEWAL

FOR READING & MEDITATION – NEHEMIAH 11:1–19

… the rest of the people cast lots to bring one
out of every ten to live in Jerusalem … (v 1)

The new fortifications needed men to guard them constantly,
and unless something was done about the problem, the city
would soon be captured by its enemies.

Some of the Jews, who clearly are more aware now of their
spiritual heritage than ever before, volunteer to move to Jerusalem,
and this evidence of patriotism and concern is obviously much
appreciated by the others. Once the plans for urban renewal are set
in motion, Nehemiah lists the families who are to make up the new
residents. There appears to have been no difficulty or disruption or
relational problems with the influx of the new people. Because of
their deep commitment to spiritual things they had the will to
work through them. But we must remember that the city under
Nehemiah was established upon sound Biblical principles, and they
were in the midst of spiritual renewal.

*Father, I am grateful that You provide me with strength. You
ask me to do nothing of which I am not capable – providing I respond to your power. Amen.*

JUDAH'S ADMINISTRATION

For reading & meditation – Nehemiah 11:20–36

The rest of the Israelites … with the priests and Levites, were
in all the towns of Judah, each on his ancestral property. (v 20)

The whole province was divided into districts, and each town
was represented by elders and leaders who were answerable
to the priests.

However the administration of Judah, we are told, was built on
a spiritual foundation, with the honour and glory of God being of
paramount importance and his justice the measure of all things.

Everyone, of course, is free to argue for the political system which
most appeals to them. I have my preference and you have yours.
What ought to be remembered, however, is that no political system
can succeed (in the fullest sense of that word) unless it is rooted in
spiritual values. A wise man said many years ago: 'Righteousness
exalts a nation, but sin is a disgrace to any people' (Prov 14:34).
Those sentiments may have dropped out of modern-day thinking,
but they remain in the Bible. They apply with equal power still.

🖙 *O God, may we in your church be the salt and light that You
have called us to be. In Jesus' Name. Amen.*

LOOK BACK TO THE PAST

These were the priests and Levites
who returned with Zerubbabel ... (v 1)

Here Nehemiah is concerned to identify the authentic traditions
of his people. We are reminded of the significance of those who
served the Lord before we arrived on the scene, and the importance
and power of godliness in the life of a nation. Many of the ordinary
people may have been ignorant of their spiritual heritage. And that
is always a tragedy. This is why the Bible constantly draws our attention to those who have gone before us. It is largely through the
labours of those who preceded us that we heard the Gospel.

The first half of the chapter makes a point by its refusal to treat
the people of the past as if they were no longer worth considering.
History may focus on the big names, but there are lots of little
names that have a big place in the heart and mind of God.

*Father, I realise that I would not belong to You now unless
others had maintained the traditions of the gospel. I am grateful
to them and to You. Amen.*

IT'S OK TO BE EXUBERANT

FOR READING & MEDITATION – NEHEMIAH 12:27–43

The sound of rejoicing in Jerusalem could be heard far away. (v 43)

When everything is ready for the dedication of the wall, Nehemiah divides the people and their leaders, the priests and the Levites into two groups. These groups, each led by a large choir, and with Ezra in one group and Nehemiah in the other, process around the wall in opposite directions and meet by the Temple. There, in the Temple, the choirs engage in a responsive anthem. The antiphonal choirs can be heard a great way off and everyone realises that the music and the singing and dancing mark a new day and a new beginning in the life of the nation.

Devotion and exuberance can belong together. Both Jewish and Church history bears witness to this. It is only when the fires in the individual heart, or that of a denomination, are dying down that convention frowns on exuberance. We probably don't see as much of it as we should.

My Father and my God, if my temperament hinders me from shouting 'Hallelujah' then help me to at least whisper it. Amen.

HOW TO SUSTAIN JOY

FOR READING & MEDITATION – NEHEMIAH 12:44–47

… all Israel contributed the daily portions
for the singers and gatekeepers. (v 47)

The words 'all Israel contributed' show us what an impact recent events have had, for the people are united in their efforts to do everything necessary to provide for those ministering in the Temple. It is interesting to note too that this is the first and only time the term 'Israel' appears in this section. Previously attention had been drawn to the sons of Benjamin and the sons of Judah, but now the focus is on 'Israel'. The parts are now swallowed up in the whole.

The teaching of this passage is not without significance for us today. When we are right with God, other things quickly fall into place. We think more in terms of the Church. We delight to minister to those who minister to us in Christ's Name and give God's Word its rightful place. Joy can never be sustained apart from that.

O God, how I long for this too – that your Church will be so one with You that everything will fall into its proper place. Help us dear Father. Amen.

OPENING UP THE WORD

FOR READING & MEDITATION – NEHEMIAH 13:1–3

On that day the Book of Moses was read
aloud in the hearing of the people. (v 1)

We do not know the precise time that the events described in
the section before us today actually took place, but we
know for certain that on a certain day the public reading of Scripture reminded the Jewish people of their special relationship with
God as his chosen ones. The passage they read was undoubtedly
Deuteronomy 23:3–6 which states categorically that no Ammo-
nite or Moabite or any of their descendants may become part of
the Lord's people. This did not mean that the Ammonites or Moa-
bites could not become converts to Judaism, but those who did not
embrace the faith had to be excluded from any and all of Israel's
activities.

Once again we notice how the public reading of the Scriptures
convicted the Jewish people of their obligations and responsibilities as God's people. We can never tell what will happen when we
open up our Bibles. But the more we do so, the more good things
are likely to happen.

*Father, once more I am reminded of the need to expose myself
to your Word on a regular basis. I dare not neglect it. Amen.*

AN INTRUDER IN GOD'S HOUSE

For reading & meditation – Nehemiah 13:4–14

Remember me for this, O my God, and do not
blot out what I have so faithfully done … (v 14)

Nehemiah has been away from Jerusalem some time (v 6). On
returning he makes the astonishing discovery that Eliashib,
the high priest, has turned a large room in the Temple into a home
for Tobiah, who was one of Nehemiah's chief enemies.

The presence of Tobiah in God's house and the negligence of
the officials had had an adverse effect on the people as they were
no longer providing for the work of the Temple. The Levites had
found it necessary to go back to toiling in their fields. Nehemiah
is deeply incensed and sets about correcting the wrongs.

How desperately we need men like Nehemiah in today's Church.
For too long we have courted the favour of the enemies of God.
There are people who need rebuking and trends that need challenging. Something drastic has to happen in God's house when the
devil lives in the vestry!

🔖 *O God, protect your people from the dangers of compromise I*
pray. This we ask in our Lord's precious Name. Amen.

A DESECRATED SABBATH

FOR READING & MEDITATION – NEHEMIAH 13:15–22

From that time on they no longer came on the Sabbath. (v 21)

Having taken care of compromise in the house of God, Nehemiah sets about rectifying another major abuse: the desecration of the Sabbath.

As he makes his way around the city and the outlying areas he sees Jews treading winepresses on the Sabbath, others bringing sacks of grain and other produce to Jerusalem in readiness for market the next day, men from Tyre actually holding an open market on Israel's holy day.

Nehemiah once again goes straight to the heart of the issue and proceeds to challenge the leaders. In case the nobles responsible remain indifferent Nehemiah steps in and commands the city gates to be closed before the Sabbath so that no merchandise can be brought into Jerusalem.

The moral decline we see today is not due entirely to the desecration of the Sabbath, of course, but there is no doubt in my mind that it has something to do with it. We either take God's commandments or take the consequences.

O Father, though the world is becoming insensitive to spiritual values and realities, let this situation never develop in your Church. Amen.

THE FINAL SCENES

FOR READING & MEDITATION – NEHEMIAH 13:23–31
Remember me with favour, O my God. (v 31)

Nehemiah's final reform concerns mixed marriages. It's the old story – forbidden things have more appeal than those given for our good.

The enthusiastic Nehemiah soon completes his reforms and once again the people settle down to a period of peace and spiritual distinctiveness.

You may have noticed that four times in this chapter his prayers begin with the word *remember*. Nehemiah lived his entire life in the presence of God and was always ready to lift his heart in prayer to Him. We learn from the life of this great and godly man that without strong and capable spiritual leadership the people of God are like sheep without a shepherd. Moral and spiritual decline then soon sets in.

To counteract this we must return to the Word of God, submit ourselves to it, confess our failures and our shortcomings and begin once again to delight in obeying the commandments of the Lord. Only then can we reflect the glory of the Lord.

☞ *O God, may this be not an end but a beginning. Give me the same burden to see broken-down walls rebuilt, and your honour fully restored. In Jesus' Name. Amen.*

NO SUBSTITUTES

Dear children, keep yourselves from idols. (v 21)

The first thing that comes to mind when *idols* are mentioned is the carved figures of pagan faiths (this is what John is referring to here), but an idol can also be, as one writer puts it, 'an expression of a universal tendency – the tendency to substitute something in the place of God'. Anything that becomes a centre of interest – greater than the interest we have in God – is an idol. Idolatry, quite simply, is substitution – substituting one thing for another. You don't need to reject God openly to be an idolater; you become one simply when you put something or someone other than God at the centre and thus marginalise Him. If He is not at the centre then He no longer controls one's life. He just faintly influences it.

Idols do more than retard our spiritual maturity; they destroy it. Mark this and mark it well: there can be no ongoing spiritual growth in the life in which idols are present.

No other gods

🖎 *Father, help me identify any idols in my life and give me the courage to tear them from their thrones. In Jesus' Name. Amen.*

'WHAT A FACE!'

The Son is ... the exact representation of his being ... (v 3)

Ask only one question about an idol to discover its validity: Is it like God in character, in power and in life? I know of nothing or no one except Jesus. Jesus is like God in every way – in character, in power and in life. As our passage puts it: 'The Son is ... the exact representation of his being.' Jesus does come between us and God as some critics suggest, however not as an idol but as Mediator because He is God. An idol cannot mediate; an idol can only misrepresent.

Behind all idolatry is the desire for God to be visible and understandable. Jesus resolves this issue by fulfilling the longing which gives rise to idolatry but in a way that no idol could ever do. Jesus gives God a face. I feel like adding *and what a face*! One small lad would get into his father's bed if he felt unwell and before dropping off to sleep would say, 'Is your face turned towards me, Daddy?' Jesus gives God a face and that face is turned towards us – always.

O Father, in knowing your Son I know You. No idols are necessary when I have the Ideal. Thank You my Father. Amen.

No other gods

SEPTEMBER 2

WHEN GOD IS OUSTED

For reading & meditation – 2 Corinthians 5:11–21

And he died for all, that those who live should
no longer live for themselves. (v 15)

The first idol I want to focus on is the *idol of the self*. Unless we depose the idol of self we will remain spiritually infantile and therefore immature.

The modern word for self is *ego* – that which is at the core of our individuality. We Christians have a different attitude to the men and women of the world. The view of the world is that we should cultivate a strong ego because (so people say) it is only then that you can give yourself to others.

But God never designed us to be ego-centred; He designed us to be God-centred. This does not mean that He wants us to have a weak ego; rather that our lives should revolve around Him instead of around our own selves. When God is not the centre then our own selves become central; we take the place of God. When we lose God we make ourselves God. There can be no greater idolatry than that.

Father, help me see clearly the freshness of your presence so that it can radiate through me. In Jesus' Name. Amen.

THE SELF – WRIT LARGE

FOR READING & MEDITATION – MATTHEW 10:32–42

Whoever finds his life will lose it, and whoever
lose his life for my sake will find it. (v 39)

When God is not the centre of our lives, the self takes over the position God originally intended for Himself.

It is a fallacy to think that when we cultivate the self then we grow. The very opposite occurs. Every self-centred person is an unhappy and unfulfilled person. He or she quickly becomes disrupted. It makes no difference if they centre upon themselves for supposedly spiritual reasons – so that they can become better Christians – for such behaviour violates the law presented in our passage today: 'Whoever finds his life will lose it.' When we focus on ourselves then we will go to pieces for life was not designed to work that way. I am convinced that more people are broken by this law than by any other thing. What happens is this: people centre on themselves and seek to have their way and then find they don't like the way they have. They run against this fundamental law: only as we lose ourselves do we find ourselves.

O God, You have wrought a law in the texture of my being. Help me run with it. In Christ's Name I pray. Amen.

THE STEPS DOWN

FOR READING & MEDITATION – JOHN 12:1–11

'Leave her alone,' Jesus replied. 'It was intended that
she should save this perfume for the day of my burial.' (v 7)

The most powerful example I know of one whose self-centredness broke the very self it was attempting to build up is Judas
Iscariot.

In Matthew 26:15 we hear the self-centred nature of his request
when asking the chief priests: 'What are you willing to give *me*?'
When anyone is motivated by 'What will you give me?' rather than
by 'What can I give you?' then his life is starting to spiral down-
wards.

Not long after Judas' betrayal of Christ his world fell apart. He
tried to save his tottering world by remorse and regret but the
world he had built for himself was not secure, not trustable. Sin
entices with false promises of happiness. The money that seemed
to matter so much was flung down and Judas went off and
hanged himself. The self that was so demanding and was more
interested in getting than giving became impossible to live with.
So he hanged the self that at first he tried to save.

*O Father, I see that this imperious demanding self will give
me trouble unless it is fully surrendered to You. Help me live as I
was intended to live. Amen.*

UNABLE TO SAY 'I'M SORRY'

FOR READING & MEDITATION – ROMANS 12:1–21

Honour one another above yourselves. (v 10)

Something I have discovered as I have made my way through life is this: the self-centred, when frustrated, turn towards themselves in self-pity. They feel that life is hard on them, and in order to deal with the pain of that they use the analgesic of self-pity. They tend to blame everything on other people or things – never themselves.

A woman I once tried to help hovered continually on the verge of a nervous breakdown. Her life was impeded by a log-jam and the chief log in the jam was self-centredness. Had she asked the Lord to help by removing that offending log then the whole jam inside would have broken loose. But she could not say the words, 'I am sorry.'

God is powerless to help those who will not yield to Him. He will not bludgeon His way into any life – He is too much of a gentleman for that. But given our consent and co-operation then there is nothing He cannot do.

Father, I would present this self of mine to You. Lift me out of myself to Yourself. In Christ's Name. Amen.

GETTING TO THE ROOT

For reading & meditation – Matthew 16:21:28

'... you do not have in mind the things
of God, but the things of men.' (v 23)

In my opinion the chief sin is the sin of self-centredness. Being
centred in self is an attempt to arrange the universe around the
wrong focal point and creates disharmony with the moral nature
of God.

Spiritual maturity has been described as 'the process by which
we are changed from an unnatural coil around the wrong centre
to a natural coil around God as the centre'. Dr E Stanley Jones put
it like this: 'Just as the fingers are rooted in the palm of the hand
so all other sins are rooted in an unsurrendered self. Why do we
lie? We think it will be of advantage to the self. Why do we become
jealous? Because the self is thwarted. Why do we become angry?
Because the self is crossed.' Counsellors should never forget this
when trying to help people. There is no point in dealing with individual sins unless one gets to the root. And the root is very often
the unsurrendered self.

Lord Jesus Christ, You have come to make me well at the very
roots of my life. I want to find myself in You and in You alone.
Amen.

SECURING SERENITY

FOR READING & MEDITATION – PSALM 138:1–8

Though the LORD is on high, he looks upon the lowly,
but the proud he knows from afar. (v 6)

If we centre ourselves on ourselves we won't like ourselves. Romans 3:16 reads: 'ruin and misery mark their ways'. This suggests that destruction and misery are not simply the result of the way of the unrighteous but inherently in their ways. The penalty for an unsurrendered self is a self you have to surrender to. If instead of God you choose yourself then you have to live with a self that is shot through with unrighteousness. When you become dependent on God then you become independent of yourself. Your self is freed from itself as it surrenders to Another.

This cannot be fully explained; it can only be experienced. A Christian woman I knew who was choked with pride and self-centredness surrendered her prideful self to God and said, 'It's so wonderful to get yourself off your own hands into the hands of God. It's so serene.' An unsurrendered self lacks serenity and is alone. Nothing backs you except yourself.

Heavenly Father, my self in my hands is a problem; in your hands it is a possibility. Thank You my Father. Amen.

NO HALF-MEASURES

FOR READING & MEDITATION – MATTHEW 12:22–37

… every city or household divided against itself will not stand. (v 25)

How do we get away from self-centredness?

One suggestion is *divide your self*. Serve two masters and get the best out of both. Be religious and get religion's consolations and be worldly and get the world's rewards. But as Jesus said in our text, a house divided against itself cannot stand.

The right way to deal with the self is to dedicate it – dedicate it to God in an act of repentance and self-surrender. Repentance because you have held on to a self that was designed to work in harmony with God and surrender because that fulfils the eternal law that you must lose yourself in order to find yourself. Until the idol of the self is dethroned we will continue to be immature personalities. So take that inmost idol and smash it once and for all by a deliberate act of self-surrender. And let there be no half-measures. A half-given self is a wholly divided self. Say to yourself, 'No half-measures for me.'

O Father, I fully repent and fully surrender. Forgive me and release me into new life and freedom. In Jesus' Name. Amen.

IDOLS LET US DOWN

FOR READING & MEDITATION – Exodus 20: 1–21

You shall have no other gods before me. (v 3)

Another idol that must be toppled if we are to move on to spiritual maturity is that of other *people*. Once people become absolutes and we look to them rather than to God we start to live dangerously.

As a young Christian I set a famous preacher of the day on a pedestal and determined to be like him. I listened to his sermons and modelled my own upon his. I studied his gestures and mannerisms and tried to copy them, even his voice. Then the news broke that he was involved in an extramarital affair. My idol tottered on its pedestal. I was devastated. The Lord said: 'Are you following him or Me?' Clearly, this preacher had come between Christ and me. I repented of my wrong actions and attitudes. To this day I remain grateful for what I learned from him, but he ceased to be an idol. Thankfully I have been free of that kind of idolatry ever since.

O Father, how sad it is that consciously or unconsciously we interpose between You and ourselves an idol. Forgive us. In Christ's Name. Amen.

THE GREAT DILEMMA

FOR READING & MEDITATION – MATTHEW 19:16–22

… love your neighbour as yourself. (v 19)

Although we must not put individuals in the place of God, nevertheless people are important to us. Though we are not to put people in the place of God we are not to live independently of each other. We are to be interdependent but should not allow that interdependence to go too far so that we then draw more from people than we do from God.

The early psychologists used to say that we have three basic instincts: the self instinct, the sex instinct and the herd instinct. We are intended to be people-oriented, to be members of society.

We too are social beings and cannot live a full life unless we form relationships. But here is the difficulty: We must relate to others, give to them and in some senses depend on them. However, if we depend on them too much we become stunted. This is indeed a real dilemma. Is there a way out of it? I believe there is.

O God our Father, teach us the way out of this dilemma. Give us your answers. In Christ's Name we ask it. Amen.

DON'T BE A PEOPLE-PLEASER

For reading & meditation – 1 John 4:7–21

There is no fear in love. But perfect love drives out fear ... (v 18)

It is right that we see ourselves as members of society but we must not be ruled by this idea. We must see that our first loyalty is to God, not the herd, and must therefore deliberately and decisively commit ourselves to that allegiance.

Many are controlled by the herd instinct to such a degree that they will never go against it – even in the interests of truth and righteousness. They are people-pleasers. However, once our loyalty is given to God we are then free to be part of the herd without being controlled by it. We will be loyal to society as long as society is loyal to God, but when the herd goes against what is right and true then we will break with it with the hope that it will call attention to the wrong which compels us to break.

With supreme allegiance to God, Jesus moved emancipated among the herd. With God our highest loyalty we are emancipated members of the herd.

Father, I belong supremely to You. Help me know when to stay with the herd and when to break with it. In Christ's Name I pray. Amen.

BEWARE OF CONTAGION

For reading & meditation – Mark 6:14–29
And he promised her with an oath, 'Whatever you
ask I will give you, up to half my kingdom.' (v 23)

When we are more dependent on others than we are on God
then our lives are thrown into confusion. The story of King
Herod makes this point most forcibly.

Herod made a foolish vow to give the daughter of Herodias anything she requested. When she asked for the head of John the
Baptist he was nonplussed, yet he ordered the head of John the
Baptist to be brought because he could not bear to think that his
guests would judge him to be a man unable to keep his word.
Thus he became the murderer of a man whom deep down he
greatly respected. And he did more than kill John the Baptist that
day; he killed his conscience.

When we start to accept the standards of the herd then before
long our Christian standards become tainted and stained. Herod's
fear of people and an undue concern for the opinions of others
brought him to the lowest point on the moral scale.

O God my Father, give me the moral courage to be inwardly
and outwardly different. Help me resist the herd when necessary.
For Christ's sake I pray. Amen.

'EVERYBODY DOES IT'

FOR READING & MEDITATION – ROMANS 15:1–13

May the God who gives endurance and encouragement
give you a spirit of unity among yourselves. (v 5)

Sometimes – to our doom – we blindly follow other people's opinions. One writer has put it like this: '"Everybody does it" is the last gurgle you can hear as men and women are submerged into the herd.' Just as we may be self-centred we can also be herd-centred. Just as self-centred people get release from themselves by surrendering themselves to God, so herd-centred people can find release from the herd by surrendering their allegiance to God.

Moving among others can release us from self-preoccupation – a very important release. If you enter society only for the purpose of getting you will get little. But if you enter in order to contribute then you will get much – as a by-product. You will lose yourself and you will find yourself again. You will grow with the growth of society. Even if others do not respond to your efforts or appreciate your contribution you will be the better for having given. In either case you win.

🔊 *Father, the herd can be either a tyranny or an opportunity. Teach me the secret of being a part and yet apart. In Jesus' Name. Amen.*

LEAN LIGHTLY ON THINGS

For reading & meditation – Hebrews 12:1–13

Let us fix our eyes on Jesus, the author
and perfecter of our faith … (v 2)

Another potential idol and one that is akin to the herd but on a
smaller scale is the group – religious or otherwise. Much
church activity nowadays involves being part of a group. Most
churches advocate small groups – house groups, fellowship groups,
growth groups.

Enjoy the group but don't become over-dependent on it. Watch
that it doesn't become an idol, for you will find that it has feet of
clay. Every group is made up of imperfect people – yourself included. I know many people who have become disillusioned because they have seen imperfection in the group of which they are
a part. Let such disillusionment toss you to Jesus' breast. Remember if you elevate either a person or a group to the level where
they command the adulation due to God alone then you are going
to be bitterly disappointed when they let you down.

We must learn to lean lightly on our group, our church or our
denomination. Our full weight must be on Jesus.

*Gracious Father, help me learn that here on a fallen earth
there is something wrong with almost everything, but in You there
is nothing wrong with anything. Amen.*

THE PUREST LOVE

FOR READING & MEDITATION – MARK 12:28–34

Love the Lord your God with all your heart
and with all your soul … (v 30)

All of us have a deep need created by God for close friendships.
Is there some way to recognise when we have crossed the line
into over-dependency?

When either party in a relationship frequently experiences jeal-
ousy, possessiveness, a desire for exclusivism, is unable to see the
other person's faults realistically or views others as a threat to the
relationship, then the signs are there that the line has been crossed.

One of the biggest problems I have to face in counselling is that
of emotional dependency. Insecure people – those who do not have
a close and dependent relationship with God – are particularly vul-
nerable. In a dependent relationship both people are looking to a
person to meet their deepest needs rather than to Jesus Christ. Thus
the other person takes the place of Jesus and becomes an idol.

Any love that comes between us and God is an illegitimate love
– even love for one's spouse. Loved ones can be idols that push
out God.

☞ *O Father, You are my first love, my purest love. From today on-
wards others shall not be an idol to me. Thank You Father. Amen.*

WATCH OUT!

FOR READING & MEDITATION – LUKE 12:13–21

Watch out! Be on your guard against all kinds of greed … (v 15)

Another idol that can easily demand our worship is *things*. There is a terrible attachment in the normal human heart to 'things'.

Almost without realising it the desire for things can grow large in our hearts and minds. Our interest in worldly goods can quickly elbow out concern about spiritual issues, and if this becomes the case we will find ourselves growing grasping, greedy and covetous.

One of the saddest states that a follower of Christ can fall into is allowing things to master his or her life. People let the desire for things master them until eventually their devotional lives become choked. A family once were on fire for God. They lost all interest in church attendance, prayer and the cultivation of their soul because they got caught up in managing a thriving business. They think they are mastering their circumstances but in fact they are being mastered by them. Things can be good servants but are terrible masters.

Lord Jesus Christ, I surrender into your hands all my desires. Things are no longer mine but Thine. Amen.

SEPTEMBER 17 | No other gods

'I AM RICHER THAN YOU'

FOR READING & MEDITATION – MATTHEW 6:19–34

Do not store up for yourselves treasures on earth ...

But store up ... treasures in heaven ... (vv 19–20)

When communism and capitalism were rival economic systems what was common to both was the belief that life consists in the possession and enjoyment of things. Their bitter quarrel was who should have them and how. Communism and capitalism say by implication: 'Things are all that matter'.

There is a story of a poor man who had just enough money to support himself in the simplest way and who spent his days helping others and ministering the love of God to them. He was once in the company of a very wealthy man who was completely immersed in his business, working all the hours that God sent, and a slave to acquisition. 'I am richer than you are,' commented the poor man. 'How can you say that?' the millionaire enquired. 'Well,' retorted the poor man, 'I have as much as I want, and you haven't.'

Things are incapable of meeting the deepest hunger of the heart. God says: 'Things are your servants, use them.'

No other gods

O God, how I long for You to deliver me from bondage to the material. In Jesus' Name I pray. Amen.

THE GREAT DANGER

FOR READING & MEDITATION – MARK 8:31–38

What good is it for a man to gain
the whole world, yet forfeit his soul? (v 36)

Jesus never suggested that things in themselves are evil. Our Lord knew a minimum of material things was necessary without which life would be difficult, if not impossible. No one can accuse the Saviour of ignoring people's needs. He fed the hungry, had a special concern for the poor and encouraged generosity among those to whom He preached. Indeed, there is evidence that He Himself lived to a great degree on the generosity of others. Christ did not scorn things, and I want it to be clear that I am not scorning them either. Could any child of God despise what God has made?

But when things become the chief purpose of living we face the terrible peril in the world today. When possessions are seen as life's greatest good, when men and women work to get rather than give, then all of life is in danger – the integrity and sound-ness of the human soul, the well-being of the community.

🕊 *Gracious and loving Father, help me find You in all my material relationships. In Christ's Name I ask it. Amen.*

THE FINAL TEST

FOR READING & MEDITATION – JEREMIAH 10:11–25

They are worthless, the objects of mockery; when
their judgement comes, they will perish. (v 15)

An idol is something which takes the place of God – a substitute. An idol such as wealth can give the appearance of security but all it does is 'break down when the test arrives'.

The inability of things to satisfy the human soul has been demonstrated in every age, yet people are still caught by the lure of acquisition. A magazine listed the ten wealthiest people in the 90s and reported, 'Every one of them has problems directly related to their riches which they would give half their riches to be able to eliminate.' Material things often bring cares and deep unease.

We must face the fact that the final 'test' of life is death. You can't take things with you. There are no pockets in a shroud and it is quite pointless arranging to have a trailer attached to your hearse. The idol of wealth is concerned with this life only. Thus it breaks down at the final test.

Father, thank You for reminding me that the things I have gathered together in this world cannot be taken with me. Amen.

A SAFE JOURNEY

FOR READING & MEDITATION – EZRA 8:15–36

... that we might humble ... ask [God] for a safe journey
for us and our children, with all our possessions. (v 21)

The main purpose of Ezra's prayer was that they might rebuild
the Temple. The matter of a safe journey for them and their
possessions was incidental. Their real concern was God's glory.

A businessman wanted me to join him in the same prayer,
asking God to provide for him and his family as He did for Ezra.

'And how do you plan to finance some aspect of the cause of
Christ?' I asked him. He had clear goals concerning what he wanted
to do for himself and his family, yet he had none concerning what
he would do with his money for God. I refused to pray in the way
he wanted and he left an angry man. Six months later he came
back with an amazing plan to give £50,000 to Christian work every
year. Then I prayed for him.

It is pointless to ask for protection for your possessions if God's
glory is not the ultimate goal.

🐾 *O God, I turn everything over to You to be used under your
guidance. We will work matters out together. Thank You, my Father.
Amen.*

AT HIS DISPOSAL

FOR READING & MEDITATION – 1 CORINTHIANS 3:1–23

… whether … the world or life or death or the present or the future – all are yours, and you are of Christ, and Christ is of God. (vv 22–23)

As we move from day to day hold our theme steadily in your mind: *keep yourselves from idols.* If things own you rather than being owned by you then they have become an idol. Tear this idol from its throne as quickly as possible because it will destroy your spiritual life and your peace with God. The real question for us all to ask ourselves right now is this: Who owns my possessions – God or myself? Whether or not we acknowledge it we do not actually own our possessions; we are only in possession of our possessions for a brief period.

If in reality we do not own our possessions then we must have the sense to say to God: 'I am not the owner; I am the ower. Teach me how to work out that relationship for Your honour and glory.'

Since we belong to God all we have belongs to God. It must therefore be at his disposal.

Lord God, I live in a world where worth is judged by possessions. Help me decide to accept the Christian way. In Jesus' Name I pray. Amen.

UNPURCHASABLE MEN

FOR READING & MEDITATION – JAMES 1:19–27

... get rid of all moral filth and the evil that is
so prevalent and humbly accept the word planted in you ... (v 21)

'Everyone has their price' is a well-known saying today, but a true Christian would reject that. The disciples of Jesus put virtue before gain and character before material benefits. Society will quickly fall apart unless it has a nucleus of men and women of integrity – 'unpurchasable' men and women.

I wish that our politicians and community leaders would make more of that than they do. Materialism has the sinister tendency to barter for the soul and filch integrity, to corrupt a person's desires and cause rot to a whole community. No wonder our Lord made this a constant emphasis in his ministry. He warned men and women by parable and by precept of the consequences of making an idol out of things and He urged people to remember the values that count as treasure in heaven.

How much do things matter in your life? Enjoy them, be truly thankful for them, but watch that they do not become your 'god'.

✎ *Lord Jesus Christ, I would have everything I own placed on the altar before You and dedicated to your purposes and your kingdom. Amen.*

VIRTUES THAT VITIATE

FOR READING & MEDITATION – COLOSSIANS 3:1–17

And whatever you do … do it all in the
name of the Lord Jesus … (v 17)

A man I knew gave substantial amounts to charitable causes. He never sought publicity and did his utmost to conceal his giving by donating the money anonymously. I admired him and mentioned my respect and appreciation for his many acts of charity. Suddenly he burst into tears. 'My motivation for donating money to charity has been more to make me feel good than to bless or minister to others. Though I have been giving my money to God and others I have not given myself.'

Our *virtues* can vitiate our spirituality. It happens when we put a quality of which we are proud in place of God. The thought that we can be in bondage to a virtue may be hard to grasp, but believe me, we can.

Be sure of this: the Almighty is ever pressing to gain possession of the inmost shrine of our being and He will not permit any intruder to occupy the centre, not even a virtue.

🖙 *O Father, help me dedicate the inmost shrine of my being to You so that not even a virtue may occupy the throne of my heart. Amen.*

PROUD OF OUR HUMILITY?

FOR READING & MEDITATION – JAMES 3:1–18

Who is wise and understanding …? Let him show it by …
deeds done in the humility that comes from wisdom. (v 13)

Today we consider the virtue of humility. Is it possible that even
humility can become an idol – a substitute for God? I am afraid
that in certain circumstances this happens.

At the end of a mid-week Bible study on humility a dear old
lady commented, 'I did so much enjoy the talk tonight. I love the
subject of humility – it is one of my best qualities.'

The virtue becomes an idol – a substitue for God.

Dr Martyn Lloyd-Jones used to say: 'The more you grow spiritually the more pride becomes a danger.' How true. Pride is a parasite that has weakened many a person's character and turned a
virtue into a vice. Let us be careful that we do not fall into the trap
of putting more confidence in our virtues than we do in God. True
humility is largely something of which we are unconscious – a
by-product of dwelling close to God. If we are conscious of it we
probably do not possess it.

O God, can it be that I am proud of my virtues? May my confidence ever be in You and not in myself. Amen.

PUNCTUALITY AND PRIDE

FOR READING & MEDITATION – EXODUS 34:1–14

Do not worship any other god, for the LORD,
whose name is Jealous, is a jealous God. (v 14)

Punctuality too can have within it the parasite of pride. Let me
illustrate.

A woman had a series of appointments with a counsellor and
always appeared in his office right on time. One day she was a
few minutes late and appeared quite frenzied. She apologised over
and over again. At last the counsellor said, 'I think we should
make your lateness the subject of our discussion today. How many
appointments have you had with me so far?' 'Eight.' 'And how
many times have you been late?' 'None, except for this occasion.'
'Do you understand what drives you to always be on time?' 'Yes,
respect for other people.'

'I accept that is a part of it, but do you think there may be a
"god" for you in this?' The counsellor's insightful question led to
some deep exchanges. The woman came to see that there was an
idol at work in her punctuality. She was relying on her own resources rather than God's.

🖙 *Heavenly Father, am I being held together by a 'god' of my
own making rather than by You? If so, help me resolve the matter.
In Jesus' Name. Amen.*

THE THIRST FOR PRAISE

FOR READING & MEDITATION – MATTHEW 6:1–4

Be careful not to do your 'acts of righteousness'
before men, to be seen by them. (v 1)

A woman in a certain church was well known for her efforts to
do good and engage in acts of kindness. Over a period of time,
however, the pastor noticed that whenever she had done some
particular deed of kindness she would report it to him and then
wait for a word of commendation. Gently and tactfully he pointed
out what he had observed. At this point she stormed out and
sadly she has never returned to the church.

There are hundreds of activities we can engage in for God and
He condescends to receive them all.

It's pleasant to be affirmed and it's encouraging when the good
things we do are acknowledged, but it is so easy for our service for
God to be spoiled by our thirst for personal praise. When our longing to be praised is greater than our desire to serve God whether
or not that service is recognised then we are dangerously close to
making it a 'god'.

*Loving Father, it is becoming increasingly clear that my de-
pendency can be misplaced. You are wounding me in order to heal
me. Thank You my Father. Amen.*

DUTIFULNESS

For reading & meditation – Psalm 1:1–6

But his delight is in the law of the LORD,
and on his law he meditates day and night. (v 2)

It is easy to put one's dependence on a virtue one has developed rather than on God. If I am asked to name the root problem in the human heart I unhesitatingly pronounce it to be *misplaced dependency*.

A fine Christian, a one-time soldier with an exceptionally keen sense of duty, was full of military virtues. They commanded everyone's admiration. He would have no trafficking with evil. 'Is it right?' he would ask of any situation, and if it was right he would do what was necessary.

It seemed almost impertinent to find fault with him. However, one day I put to him the suggestion that he might be governed more by a sense of duty than dependence on God. He saw it at once and prayed, 'I don't want to be held together by duty; I want to be held together by You.' He continued to be a dutiful person but his dutifulness came from his God-dependence rather than self-dependence.

🕊 *O Father, I want nothing to come between You and me – not even a virtue. In Christ's Name. Amen.*

SOMETHING MISSING!

FOR READING & MEDITATION – PROVERBS 3:1–12

Trust in the LORD with all your heart and lean
not on your own understanding ... (v 5)

Even the virtue of self-discipline can become a 'god' to us. A
Christian author suggested: 'Discipline is what makes makes
dependable disciples.' I find something missing here.

Discipline is definitely needed in our lives if we are to be good
disciples of the Master. Very often 'free grace' has been preached in
such a way that character has been weakened. Paul warns against
this in these words: 'You, my brothers, were called to be free. But
do not use your freedom to indulge the sinful nature ...' (Gal 5:13).
Here liberty had become licence. Discipline was needed.

But we must be careful here for once again it is possible for us
to fasten on to a virtue to such an extent that it becomes the 'god'
that governs our life. And, as we have been seeing, nothing must
take the place of God, not even a virtue. Respectfully I complete
the author's statement: *dependency* plus discipline makes dependable disciples.

🕊 *Father, the strength for a disciplined life must come from You.
Make me a dependent as well as a dependable disciple. Amen.*

INDULGENT PRAYING

FOR READING & MEDITATION – MATTHEW 6:5–15

And when you pray, do not be like the hypocrites … (v 5)

A friend confronted me following a prayer meeting during which I had prayed a number of times. Gently and lovingly he said: 'Sometimes you leave other people not wanting to follow you in prayer because they may not have such skill with words as you do. Is there a 'god' in this for you?' I was devastated. 'Leave me. I must examine my heart.' At first I could not conceive that my public prayers were exercises in self-indulgence and was deeply disappointed with my friend's analysis. But the Holy Spirit confirmed my friend's loving confrontation: 'He's right.' My reaction then was, 'I'll never pray again in public.' But that was childish and immature. God's grace helped me pray simpler prayers in public with less dependency on my vocabulary and more dependency on God.

If prayerfulness is one of your Christian qualities and you are one of God's intercessors then rejoice in it. But don't depend on your prowess in prayer. Depend only on God.

O Father, give me greater prowess in prayer. But let me depend fully and only on Thee. In Jesus' Name. Amen.

SELF-ATONEMENT

For reading & meditation – Romans 5:1–11

... we also rejoice in God through our Lord Jesus Christ,
through whom we have now received reconciliation. (v 11)

The next idol posing a great hindrance to spiritual maturity is
the idol of penance. Many involve themselves in an act of penance in order to clear the guilt that has arisen in their soul over
some spiritual violation; they depend on the act of penance rather
than on Christ's atoning sufferings on Calvary and thus substitute
their own atonement for his. Penance then becomes an idol – a
substitute for the real thing.

This tendency to make amends for one's wrongdoing must be
watched most carefully for I have seen many Christians fall into
the trap of believing that they can atone for sin by an act of penance. They are therefore trusting in their own efforts rather than
the atonement which Christ procured for them on the cross. This
is why the great preacher George Whitefield once said to a congregation: 'Our very penance needs to be repented of.' It does if it depends more on self than the Saviour.

*Father, your Son's atonement means that there is no need for
self-atonement. May I ever revel and rejoice in this. In Jesus' Name.
Amen.*

AN ESCAPE FROM GUILT

FOR READING & MEDITATION – PSALM 32:1–11

When I kept silent, my bones wasted
away through my groaning all day long. (v 3)

It might be helpful to note the various ways in which people can
deal with unconfessed guilt. Counsellors have often commented
on the interesting fact that when a man or woman falls into sin
and a sense of guilt begins to spread through the personality some
inner mechanism goes to work to help them escape it or dissolve
it. Some (albeit unconsciously) try to escape from guilt by developing an illness. The illness is the soul's way of saying, 'If you
won't deal with the discomfort in your soul then deal with it in
your body.'

A number of commentators believe that the psalm we have read
today was written by David before he confessed his adultery with
Bathsheba. Clearly he speaks of the physical effects of his unconfessed sin (vv 3–4). Was his physical discomfort the off-loading of
his soul's discomfort? I cannot say for sure, but as I have seen this
condition in many people I have to conclude, yes.

No other gods

OCTOBER 2

Father, save me from trying to escape from the consequence of
evil. I want no escape routes, no alibis, just You. Amen.

OTHER FORMS OF RETREAT

For reading & meditation – Luke 15:15–32

... the younger son ... set off for a distant country
and there squandered his wealth in wild living. (v 13)

A young girl was found wandering the streets of London in a state of amnesia. A follow-up report stated that the girl came from a respectable and religious home and because she was feeling very guilty because she had taken to drugs amnesia had become her attempt to deal with the guilt that arises in her soul from unconfessed sin.

This illustration is more the exception than the rule, but I have seen so many different forms of retreat to convince me the soul is adept at helping us escape from the feelings that arise whenever a moral principle has been violated.

Some try to escape in more overt ways, for instance by drinking alcohol to dull the conscience. But over every escape route is a sign that reads, 'No way through.' Guilt can be assuaged but it can never be properly removed through self-pity, illness or any other form of escapism. You can't make a halfway house a home.

Father, help us to experience release from guilt through full confession and repentance. Help us face reality. In Jesus' Name. Amen.

OCTOBER 3 | *No other gods*

THE CIRCLE OF OFFENCE

For reading & meditation – Matthew 5:21–26

Therefore, if you … remember that your brother has something
against you … go and be reconciled to your brother … (vv 23–24)

Regarding the way in which the soul seeks to escape from inner guilt, I quote the psychologist Carl Jung: 'It is only with the help of confession that I am able to throw myself into the arms of humanity, freed at last from the burden of moral exile.'

I would have preferred it if he had said: 'It is only with confession that I am able to throw myself into the arms of God and man, and ask for forgiveness and restoration.'

Don't be put off by the phrase 'and man'. If someone has committed an offence against God and another person then both God and the other person must be approached. The principle I have always followed is this: if the violation is against God and God alone then seek his forgiveness only. If it is against God and someone else then seek the forgiveness of God and the individual. Limit the confession to the circle of offence.

🕯 *O Father, help me understand this principle of limiting the confession to the circle of offence so that I can resolve issues in a Biblical way. Amen.*

JONAH – THE IMPENITENT

FOR READING & MEDITATION – JONAH 1:1–17

Pick me up and throw me into the sea …

and it will become calm. (v 12)

Probably one of the clearest illustrations of someone resorting to penance, as opposed to repentance, is Jonah. Realising that Jonah was running away from God, the sailors asked Jonah how the sea could calm down. Jonah replied: 'Pick me up and throw me into the sea and it will become calm.' He proposed self-punishment as atonement.

I have seen people approach a church on their knees as an act of penance. These people do not understand the difference between penance and repentance. Penance is an attempt to make atonement for sin by an act which often causes suffering. Repentance is sorrow for sin leading to a turning away from it and the discovery of release in Christ.

There is a genuine place for penance in the Christian life – the story of Zaccheus shows this. But far too often penance is a substitute for repentance. This is how it was (I believe) with Jonah. He mistook remorse for repentance – a mistake made by millions.

🖝 *O Father, teach me the difference between penance and repentance in the Christian life. In Christ's Name I pray. Amen.*

DID JONAH REPENT?

FOR READING & MEDITATION – JONAH 2:1–10

I said, I am cast out of thy sight; yet I
will look again toward thy holy temple. (v 4)

Jonah was willing to go overboard but not to go to Nineveh. There
is something about human nature that makes us want to *do*
something to remedy our spiritual deficiencies rather than trust in
the grace and power of God. We use high-sounding words, pray
eloquently, involve ourselves in charitable acts (all good things in
themselves), but our intention is to persuade God that He should
listen to us when we should be throwing ourselves upon his mercy
and grace.

We have to recognise that in ourselves we are powerless to atone.
Though we must do what we can to right wrongs, the action of
putting things right must not be seen as atonement. God has provided atonement for us through Christ's redeeming sacrifice on the
cross and we must be careful that we do nothing to bypass that,
either in thought or in deed.

An act of penance may be needed in addition to repentance but
must never replace it.

*Father, your blood alone provides cleansing for my soul. Help
me to grasp this fact. In Jesus' Name. Amen.*

'LOOK WHAT YOU MADE ME DO!'

Jonah … waited to see what would happen to the city. (v 5)

Jonah is addressed the second time by God: 'Go to the great city of Nineveh and proclaim to it the message I give you' (3:2). So Jonah went there. He went outwardly but not inwardly. There is no evidence of compassion in his heart. He not only wanted to inflict pain on himself; he wanted others to suffer too.

The unrepentant always blame others. In this case Jonah blamed God. And watch how he continued to punish himself. He wanted God to take away his life. This put him in control. He was the one giving the orders.

When there is insincere repentance then the tendency is to rely on substitutes, to hop from one subterfuge to another. Jonah wanted to die because he had never died to Jonah. He had never truly repented, I believe. When the curtain falls Jonah is still running. Be careful that when the curtain falls on your life your situation is not like that of Jonah.

My Father, unless I know what true repentance is I can move from one subterfuge to another. May nothing ever come between me and You, dear Lord. Nothing. Amen.

'A CELESTIAL SANTA CLAUS'

FOR READING & MEDITATION – HEBREWS 11:1–10

… anyone who comes to him must believe that he exists … (v 6)

Many Christians are *clinging to a wrong concept of God.* They form a concept of Him that is more acceptable to them, little realising that by doing so they are actually substituting imagination for revelation, and that is idolatry.

'Tell me, how do you see God?' is a question I have often put to believers down the years. The replies have been revealing. 'I see God,' said one man, 'as standing over me, ready and willing at any given moment to pull me out of trouble.' 'And does He?' I enquired. 'Of course,' was the reply, 'every time.'

I happened to know he was in trouble that very moment – deep financial trouble – and his business was on the verge of bankruptcy. He couldn't live with the reality of a God who might allow his business to go bankrupt so he retreated into denial. He wanted a God who kept him *out* of trouble, not *in* it – a celestial Santa Claus, an idol.

No other gods

OCTOBER 8

🖙 *Gracious and loving heavenly Father, help me never to place my imagination above your revelation. Amen.*

METAL AND MENTAL IMAGES

FOR READING & MEDITATION – JEREMIAH 10:1–16

… they cut a tree out of the forest, and
a craftsman shapes it with his chisel. (v 3)

Idolatry can take the form of placing imagination above God's revelation. People use their imagination to create the most astonishing gods and thereby reveal their perception of them.

'But hasn't God given us the gift of imagination?' says someone. Yes, God has given us imagination, but we are fallen beings and our imagination can easily become warped and twisted. When we allow our imagination to follow our fantasies then we develop a concept of God that is not only wide off the mark but idolatrous.

In his denunciation of idolatry, whether the image being venerated is a metal or a mental one, God declares: 'Don't miscalculate my reaction. I, the Lord your God, am a jealous God.' With all the intensity and integrity of his being He insists on his rightful place at the centre of the universe and on the throne of his people's hearts. He will resist with omnipotent power anything that seeks to prevent him occupying that central position.

OCTOBER 9 | *No other gods*

 O God, may I be passionate about making sure that there is no god in my life except the one true and living God. In Jesus' Name. Amen.

IN SPIRIT AND IN TRUTH

For reading & meditation – John 4:1–24

God is spirit, and his worshippers must
worship in spirit and in truth. (v 24)

When we do not allow our concept of God to be shaped by the Scriptures, our spiritual lives are deeply affected and we are hindered from moving towards maturity.

What is the truth about God? The truth is that He doesn't always deliver us from trouble though of course He promises to stay with us in it. He doesn't intervene to stop little children to be sexually or physically abused, permits Christian businesses to go bankrupt, lets bad things happen to good people, and so on.

Some Christians are not prepared to face these hard facts. We need not dwell on them but we must face them otherwise we are in danger of forming a concept of God which makes us feel more comfortable but is a false one. Accepting God as He is means facing up to the fact that some things He docs are beyond explanation and are a complete and utter mystery. But we decide to trust him nevertheless.

☞ *O God, even though I do not have explanations for the strange things You allow to happen I recognise that I must decide to trust You. Amen.*

TRUE WORSHIP

For we cannot do anything against the truth,
but only for the truth. (v 8)

If we find it difficult to accept God as He is and thus change our concept of him so that we can live more comfortably, we are totally destroying the reality of who God is. Though we cannot explain why He allows certain things to happen in the way He does, nevertheless we trust him. Maybe some things are a mystery that only God can comprehend and to try to explain them would mystify us even more.

CS Lewis also said this about worship: 'In the process of worship God communicates his presence to men.' God cannot fully come in to us except through worship and we cannot fully communicate with God unless we worship in spirit and in truth. Note my emphasis on the word truth. No truth – no worship. We remain stunted and immature if we refuse to face reality. Sometimes we might wish God would act differently but we must watch that a wish does not develop into a demand.

O Father, You mean more to me than anything or anyone. Help me get this matter of worship right. In Jesus' Name. Amen.

FASTENING ONTO A FANTASY

FOR READING & MEDITATION – 1 JOHN 1:1–10

If we claim to be without sin, we deceive
ourselves and the truth is not in us. (v 8)

In a section concentrating on the reality of God we need to admit
we are sinners. The purpose is to emphasise the importance of
admitting to the truth whether that truth be about our own in-
nate evil or the truth about God. If we refuse to admit that we are
sinners, then we live in a world of illusion and truth becomes a
stranger to us.

Seeing things not as they are but as we would like them to be,
brings about a diminution of our personalities. A serious thing
takes place when we do not accept God as He is but seek to change
Him into someone with whom we can live more comfortably: we
put in God's place an image we have manufactured ourselves. Do
I need to labour the point? It is fastening upon a fantasy. There is
a word for it. I hope the word is not becoming so familiar that it
is losing its seriousness. The word is *idolatry*.

*O Father, your Word cuts deep into my spirit. If there is no
greater sin than idolatry, keep me free of all idols. In Jesus' Name.
Amen.*

THREE WAYS TO 'SEE' GOD

FOR READING & MEDITATION – JOHN 1:1–18

No one has ever seen God, but God the One and Only, who is at the Father's side, has made him known. (v 18)

We cannot worship God properly unless we accept Him as He is. We can admire a caricature but we can't worship it, for true worship, according to CS Lewis's definition implies a two-way process: 'In the process of worship God communicates himself to men.' We will not be able to work or witness for God either unless we accept Him as He is.

A Jehovah's Witness visiting my home portrayed God as cold, clinical, distant and grudgingly communicative. After they had left I gave thanks to God for the Holy Spirit who reveals to us God's warmth and beauty and loveliness.

Inevitably the way we see God will govern the way we will talk about him. Our perceptions determine our communications. How do you see God? There are only three ways we can see Him. One, as He is. Two, as we imagine Him to be. Three, as we would like Him to be. What is your concept of the Deity?

O God my Father, I hope I am in touch with reality as I talk to others about You. Help me evaluate this. In Jesus' Name. Amen.

JESUS' OTHER NAME

'I am the way and the truth and the life. No one
comes to the Father except through me.' (v 6)

We will never have a clear concept of God until we have a
clear concept of Jesus. How true what E Stanley Jones said:
'Jesus takes the place of idols.' When we have Jesus the need for
idols drops away. Often people worship an idol because they want
something that is get-at-able, tangible, approachable. Jesus is all
these. He is *Immanuel*, God with us.

We have been talking a good deal about reality. God did not give
us a proposition in order to explain reality; He gave us a Person.
And what a Person! Jesus is the way that can be trodden. He trod
it. Jesus is the truth. His truth rings true everywhere. Jesus is the
life that can be lived. He lived it. When reality renders its verdict it
points to Jesus.

Do you want to know what God is like? Then look at Jesus.
Nothing can be truer than this final quote from E Stanley Jones:
'Reality – whose other name is Jesus.'

*Lord Jesus, blessed Reality, you have made the complex sim-
ple, the hidden known, the unknowable plain. I am so thankful.
Amen.*

GOD AT OUR LEVEL

FOR READING & MEDITATION – 1 KINGS 8:22–30

O LORD, God of Israel, there is no God like you
in heaven above or on earth below … (v 23)

Another form of idolatry is that of *reductionism* – bringing God down to our level. This kind of idolatry imposes limits on divine transcendence and contributes to the shrinking of God in our minds. We thus substitute a lesser god for the true God.

When Solomon built the Temple he felt awestruck by the magnificent structure until God deigned to enter it. Then Solomon said: 'The heavens, even the ... highest heaven, cannot contain you. How much less this temple I have built!' (v 27).

There are some Christians who like to think of their church building as the place where God is confined because they can then keep Him in there, visit Him once a week like a sick relative, and run their lives the way they want to. This destroys reverence by making God less than He is. It is true that He came down to our level in the incarnation, but immanence was not achieved at the cost of transcendence.

🐦 *Father, don't let me ever lose my balance with regard to these two truths immanence and transcendence. In Jesus' Name. Amen.*

A GREAT MYSTERY

He who descended is the very one who ascended higher than
all the heavens, in order to fill the whole universe. (v 10)

God's coming to this earth in the form of a man is the event
that marks Christianity as being distinct from every other
faith. All other religions are mankind's attempt to climb to God.
The incarnation is God's descent to us.

When He came to earth as a man God did not bring a religion
to set alongside other religions – one a little better, more moral,
more spiritual. He came to set the gospel over against human
need whether that need be in followers of this religion or that
religion or of no religion.

The Son of God became the Son of Man in order that the sons
of men might become the sons of God. And here is the mystery
– our text focuses on it: our Lord who became man ascended to
the Father and now as a man (remember that) He fills the whole
universe. Because of the incarnation his immanence is incontro-
vertible. And so also is his transcendence.

🙵 *Loving Father, You are small enough to fill my heart but big
enough to fill the entire universe. I cannot fully understand it but
I stand upon it. Amen.*

THE FINE LINE

For reading & meditation – James 4:1–17

… you ought to say, 'If it is the Lord's will,
we will live and do this or that.' (v 15)

Each culture and generation makes its own attempt to reduce God to a size where He can be manipulated. In Britain many believe in God's existence (recent research said 70 per cent) but see him as an affectionate uncle who pats us on the head and instructs, 'Enjoy yourself, but be careful.'

We must recognise that God does indeed concern himself with his people and is interested in blessing them, sometimes in material ways. My concern is the tendency to think that they can have God under their control.

Prayer says, 'Lord, I would like this to happen, but I understand You see things from a different perspective so I submit everything to your judgement.' Demandingness says, 'Lord, this is what I want to happen and so let it be according to the word of faith that is now on my lips.' There is a very fine line between faith and demandingness and, in my opinion, many Christians are not able to recognise it.

O Father, much of what I regard as faith is based on my own desires and demands. Help me have the right kind of faith. Amen.

GOD IN A BOX

FOR READING & MEDITATION – 2 SAMUEL 6:1–11

... Uzzah reached out and took hold of the ark of God ...
The LORD's anger burned against Uzzah ... (vv 5–6)

What an extraordinary thing to happen. A man accompanying the ark of God tries to steady it when it is in danger of crashing to the floor and is struck dead by the Lord.

I believe Uzzah was guilty of having a limited view of God's transcendence. If we could have looked into his heart I think we might have found that his understanding of God was of a being confined to a box. The ark contained some sacred objects: the original ten commandments, a pot of manna and Aaron's rod that budded. It played a miraculous part in the wanderings in the wilderness, the crossing of Jordan, the fall of Jericho. However, although the ark was a symbol of God's presence, that did not mean He was confined to it. I think Uzzah saw it in that way and missed the point.

Nothing insults God more than when we assume that we can carry Him rather than accepting that He carries us.

Father, drive deep into my soul the conviction that the greatest insult I can give You is to treat You as if You can be managed. In Jesus' Name. Amen.

WHO CARRIES WHO?

FOR READING & MEDITATION – ISAIAH 46:1–13

I am God, and there is no other; I am God,
and there is none like me. (v 9)

When we think we are in control of God then we are nothing more than idolaters. We are attempting to manage the unmanageable, to control the uncontrollable.

The people of Isaiah's day carried their idols around with them and experienced spiritual death as a result. Wherever they went the Babylonians carried their idols with them. In contrast, Isaiah reminds his hearers that God has carried them since their birth. 'I am he who will sustain you ... and I will carry you' (v 4).

Note the phrase again: 'I will carry you.' If our understanding of God is that we can carry Him then we are attempting to be in control. Perhaps I want to make God manageable so that I can put Him where I want Him and where He won't intrude too much on my life. If I am seeking to control God then I am trying to make myself God. Think about that, and drop the attempt as quickly as possible.

O loving Father, the thought that I may be taking your place horrifies me. Let your Spirit probe my heart. In Jesus' Name. Amen.

SUBTLE SELF-DEIFICATION

FOR READING & MEDITATION – ISAIAH 40:18–31

Do you not know? Have you not heard?
The LORD is the everlasting God ... (v 28)

A certain minister came close to deifying himself. He believed that his church was the only one that preached the gospel and that he was the only minister in his town who lived according to the standards of Scripture. He became terribly upset when people would not leave their churches and join his church. The church officers decided they would do and say nothing but trust the Lord to bring matters to a right conclusion. That was a mistake. Soon many of the church officers began to share the minister's vision.

Fortunately a retired minister who lived in the town visited the church one day and sensing what was going on stood up at the end of a service and lovingly and gently shared his concerns. This triggered a time of deep heart-searching among the church officials and the congregation. That church and its minister was saved from spiritual disaster.

We are not God. If we think we are then God help us.

🐦 *Father, thinking I am God is utterly offensive, but I see it can happen very subtly. Help me Father. In Jesus' Name. Amen.*

'BEWARE OF GOD'

For reading & meditation – Hebrews 12:14–29
... for our 'God is a consuming fire.' (v 29)

Signs everywhere are warning us, 'Beware of Pickpockets', 'Beware of Floods', and so on. Sometimes I think to myself: I wonder what would happen if our churches had a sign outside that said 'Beware of God'. I am just wondering what the effect would be.

I believe one of the greatest needs in the contemporary Christian Church is to catch a new vision of the transcendence of God. We are so taken up with his immanence – His nearness and availability – that we tend to ignore the fact of his transcendence.

Everything in our churches is geared towards keeping things working well.

God is not someone to be managed but someone who is high and lifted up and who deserves to be worshipped. We need to be delivered from the idolatry of trying to manage him and instead let him manage us. 'Without real transcendence,' says Dr Larry Crabb, 'there is no weighty God to fall before, only a co-operative God to celebrate.'

O Father, may I hold these two great truths – immanence and transcendence – in perfect balance. For Jesus' sake. Amen.

A SUBSTITUTE LOVE

FOR READING & MEDITATION – LUKE 10:25–37
He answered: 'Love the Lord your God …
and, 'Love your neighbour … (v 27)

If divine love, *agape* love, is the highest manifestation of the character of God and is the fuel on which our lives are meant to run then dependence on a lesser love is one of the most serious idolatries of all.

Our maturity, therefore, is measured by our maturity in love. And one of the biggest hindrances to maturity is moving through life with a greater dependence on human love than on the divine.

When an expert in the law stood up and asked Jesus what he had to do to inherit eternal life, Jesus did not say 'You must be just'. He sounded a clarion note: 'You shall love.' The ages were thirsting for that word for from the beginning that is what we were made to do – to love. The first obligation God lays on every one of us is to love. And not simply to love in the way we understand love but as God loves.

Gracious Father, life must be lived with agape or else forever remain immature. Grant me your power and presence as I continue. In Jesus' Name. Amen.

AN ETHICAL REVOLUTION

FOR READING & MEDITATION – 1 CORINTHIANS 13:1–13

Love does not delight in evil but rejoices with the truth. (v 6)

We continue exploring the fact that the substitution of human love for the divine is a form of idolatry. But exactly what do we mean by 'love'?

The ancient Greeks used the word *eros* to express the idea of love for human beings and also love for God, but Christians adopted the Greek word *agape* and gave it a distinctively Christian sense. That word, when filled with Christian meaning, introduces the most revolutionary idea ever presented to the mind of man. Anders Nygren, a devout Christian and an authority on the Greek language, says: 'The Christian idea of love ... involves a revolution in ethical outlook without parallel in the history of ethics.' Strange though it may seem, the revolution of which he speaks is scarcely mentioned in the traditional histories of ethics. As Christians we simply must understand this revolution arising from the Christian takeover of the word *agape* so that it grips and controls us as it did the Early Church.

O God, guide me, my Father, into a true understanding of what it means to love – from the divine point of view. In Jesus' Name. Amen.

EROS AND AGAPE

FOR READING & MEDITATION – PHILIPPIANS 2:1–18

... make my joy complete by being like-minded,
having the same love, being one in spirit and purpose. (v 2)

The difference between *eros* and *agape* is put most clearly in the parallels given by Anders Nygren.

Eros is acquisitive desire and longing; *Agape* is sacrificial giving. *Eros* is man's way to God; *Agape* is God's way to man. *Eros* is egocentric; *Agape* is unselfish. *Eros* seeks to gain its life; *Agape* lives the life of God therefore dares to 'lose it'. *Eros* is primarily man's love; *Agape* is primarily God's love. *Eros* is the will to get and possess; *Agape* is freedom in giving.

What strikes you? *Eros*, generally speaking, is the love that loves for what it can gain from that love. It turns everything – even God – into a means to an end. *Eros* loves because it sees in its object of love something that can bring satisfaction in return. Here the issues are drawn. As Christians we must decide on which side we will line up for we have to be on one side or the other.

🍃 *My Father and my God, help me line up on the side of agape. I want to love as You love. In Christ's Name I ask it. Amen.*

THREE VIEWS OF THE SOUL

FOR READING & MEDITATION – ROMANS 3:1–20

All have turned away, they have together become worthless … (v 12)

There are three views concerning the soul. Some claim the soul is naturally Christian. Tertullian, one of the Church Fathers, first said: the soul is naturally Christian. Others believe the soul is naturally pagan. Still others maintain the soul is half-Christian and half-pagan. I vote with Tertullian: *the soul is naturally Christian*. It is made for God and functions effectively only when He is in it. There is something in us all that feels evil is evil; we witness to it as being unnatural.

In *The Screwtape Letters* by CS Lewis a senior devil writing to a junior devil says: 'We work under a cruel handicap. Nothing is naturally on our side. Everything has to be twisted before it is of any use to us.' The love that God put into us at the beginning has been twisted by sin. We can still love but not in the way God loves. Our love needs a homecoming. It needs to be converted.

Father, I see that I am natural only when I am in You. I meet my self, my real self, in You. Thank You my Father. Thank You. Amen.

'CONVERSION OF OUR LOVES'

FOR READING & MEDITATION – JOHN 21:15–25

Again Jesus said, 'Simon son of John, do you truly love me?' (v 26)

Because the love God put in us at the beginning has been twisted, our love needs to be converted. But how? Can *eros* be changed into *agape*?

I believe *eros* can be converted, not by effort but by self-surrender. When self-surrender takes place then the love which is inherently in the self is untangled from the self and fastened onto God who is *Agape*. The fact is, as the missionary Norman Grubb put it, that *'Conversion is the conversion of our loves'.* We have loved the wrong things for the wrong reason, he claimed, and for the wrong ends. In other words, love has been perverted – perverted from *agape* to *eros*. If evil is perversion of the good then conversion is conversion from perversion. Those who are converted, truly converted, begin to love the right things for the right reasons and for the right ends. Loving with the right kind of love is agape. It is what we were made for. Nothing more, nothing less.

O God, my heart longs to love as it was made to love, but sin still dwells in me. Set me free, dear Lord. In Jesus' Name. Amen.

PUT OUT YOUR CANDLES

FOR READING & MEDITATION – 1 JOHN 4:7–21

We love because he first loved us. (v 19)

We were never intended to be the centre of the universe. God is the centre and in him we are right-centred. Therefore what was perverted has been converted. When we see and feel *agape* we can no longer be content with *eros*. We put out our candles for the sun has come up.

But isn't *agape* too high for us to attain? How can we love as God loves? Isn't that just for saints and exceptional people? The answer is found in our text for today: 'We love because He first loved us.' Note the word *because*. To have God's love in us requires not striving but receiving.

When we focus on the fact that we are loved by the world's greatest Lover and open ourselves to that love it flows like Niagara's waters into our souls. You don't need to strive; you simply have to let it come in. Open your eyes and the light comes in. Open your heart and love comes in.

🕊 *O Father, your love is the spring of my love. Your agape becomes agape in me. Help me open myself to it. In Jesus' Name. Amen.*

LOVING GOD FOR 'ME'

FOR READING & MEDITATION – 2 CORINTHIANS 5:11–21

For Christ's love compels us, because we are
convinced that one died for all ... (v 14)

In living the Christian life our dependency must not be on our own
resources but on those made available to us in God and through
Christ. Maturity is where we place our dependency. And dependency
on our human love instead of on God's love is idolatry.

Human love loves for what it can gain. It loves people for what
they can give in return. We love others because we see in them
something that can bring satisfaction. God too can be loved for
what He gives rather than for who He is. We make him a means
to our end. He saves us from trouble, heals our sicknesses, gives
us success in life, and provides us with a heaven hereafter. The
Almighty is therefore well worth serving.

When we approach God like this and daily function from this
perspective we are substituting for *agape* love our own self-centred love. This substitution is one of the greatest idolatries of all.

*Father, I see my greatest danger is not in being anti-Christian
but sub-Christian. Help me organise my life around You, not myself. Help me in Christ's Name. Amen.*

NOTHING HIGHER

FOR READING & MEDITATION – JOHN 15:1–17
'My command is this: Love each other as I have loved you.' (v 12)

When the Bible tells us 'God is love' it is making the point that He is love *essentially*. Therefore He can do nothing without love being his motivation and method. There can be no movement on God's part without it being governed by love. He would violate His own nature if He did anything that was not motivated by love. Love is even what lies behind His anger.

When God made us He made us like himself and stamped deep within us the same kind of love as He himself possesses – *agape* love. Sadly, Adam and Eve separated themselves from God and, once they had, their *agape* turned to *eros*.

However, God sent his Son into our world, and demonstrated for us what *agape* is really like. In our text we find Jesus saying: 'Love each other as I have loved you.' Jesus filled the word love with the purest and deepest love this planet has ever seen. There is nothing higher.

Lord Jesus Christ, I look into your face and I know now the meaning of love. May I love others with the love that You have for me. Amen.

MISREPRESENTING GOD

FOR READING & MEDITATION – JOHN 13:18–38

'By this all men will know that you are my disciples,
if you love one another.' (v 35)

When we attempt to function day by day on *eros* love – a love that is largely shot through with self-centredness – we have a misplaced dependency, another term for idolatry.

When we, as Christians, settle for anything less than *agape* love, we are displaying an image of God that is not true. We are misrepresenting God. If we say we love but all the world sees is a love that is self-centred, egocentric and is out for what it can get, we are conveying that God has that attitude. Instead the world should see us exhibiting a love that says, 'I don't want to get, I want to give.'

Anything less or other than *agape* is a substitution. We are not meant to function by or depend upon love that is not *agape* love. Let us have done with the idolatry of a substitute love and allow God's *agape* to penetrate our souls until we too are filled with all the fullness of God.

No other gods

Father, I renounce the idolatry of substitute love and come to You for release, forgiveness and wholeness. In Jesus' Name. Amen.

OCTOBER 30

'HIM ONLY'

Then the devil left him, and angels came and attended him. (v 11)

There are many more things which can wrongly claim our affection than the eight issues I have focused on. Status for example, work, the cause of Christ rather than Christ Himself, ambition, our own talents and abilities, seeking spiritual experiences rather than the knowledge of God, also, for example, nationalism, race, religious ceremonies and so on.

Our passage today shows what happens when we surrender fully to Christ and confess Jesus as our only Lord. When Jesus said to the devil following the third temptation 'Serve him only' the devil, we are told, left him. The devil could not stand the 'him only' attitude and decision.

So from now on let there be no trucking with idols, no substitutes, no lesser gods, no god-shelf on which Jesus stands as one among many other gods. Sweep every idol from your life. There must be no substitute for Him. Let your resolve be 'Him only'. Make these powerful words of the hymnist your constant prayer:

The dearest idol I have known,
What'er that idol be,
Help me to tear it from its throne,
And worship only Thee.
Amen.

OCTOBER 31 | No other gods

UNSINKABLE!

FOR READING & MEDITATION – 2 CORINTHIANS 4:1–18
'We are hard pressed on every side, but not
crushed; perplexed, but not in despair …' (v 8)

One of the greatest of our problems is that of crumbling values. Truth is seen by many in today's world to be subjective. Engage a non-Christian in a discussion about Christian issues and you are likely to hear the statement, 'That may be the truth for you, but I operate from a different truth.' Generally speaking, our age has lost its sense of God, and all life feels the shattering effect of this loss.

How do we as Christians stand up to such an age as this? Where do we find the inner strength to face the challenges of these fast-changing times?

We find it, of course, in God. But can we realise God within us in such a way that no matter what occurs on the outside, we will remain strong and secure on the inside? If we can't, we are sunk; if we can, we will be unsinkable. Walk with me and I will show you we can.

My Father and my God, my heart is open to all You want to teach me. Lead on and I will follow. In Jesus' Name. Amen.

Staying spiritually strong

NOVEMBER 1

'SETTLING DOWN IN GOD'

For reading & meditation – Isaiah 26:1– 6

You will keep in perfect peace him whose
mind is steadfast, because he trusts in you. (v 3)

How well do you know God? Well enough to stand up to anything that comes with inner strength? Or, to put it another way, well enough to rest your whole weight on Him? There can be no enjoyment of a flight, or of life as a whole, unless you learn to put your whole weight down.

Inner strength can come from many things. Some may find a type of inner fortitude from studying relaxation techniques, transcendental meditation, and so on. But this world provides nothing on which we can fully rest our weight.

The Quakers used to talk about 'settling down in God'. Have you learned to 'settle down in God', to trust Him so completely that no matter what happens on the surface of life the depths remain tranquil? An ocean appears turbulent when waves are tumbling and crashing on the surface, but a few hundred feet below all is calm. Can we be like that? In God we can.

O Father, teach me all I need to know to remain tranquil when around me the waves of life are turbulent. In Jesus' Name. Amen.

APPROACHES TO INNER PEACE

FOR READING & MEDITATION – ISAIAH 59:1–8

The way of peace they do not know;
there is no justice in their paths. (v 8)

In an attempt to find inner strength we look at different approaches. The Greeks' quest for inner strength was expressed in Stoicism which tries to gain inner strength by shutting out all feelings – even love and pity.

China has what is called 'the superior man' – the man who tries to achieve inner strength and poise by giving way to no circumstance about him. If soup is spilled on him, for instance, he is not expected to remove it until he has withdrawn from the presence of others. He should be unmoved and show no emotion.

Islam has a quite different method of obtaining inner strength: the belief that everything that happens to you is the will of God, and you should accept it. However, God does not will everything. He does not will wrongdoing. Islam fails to differentiate between what God wills and what He allows. This quest of Islam may produce passivity, but not true poise. There must be another way.

My Father, I am on a quest to obtain inner peace that is so important that I must not fail to find the way. Help me my Father. Amen.

SOME MODERN APPROACHES

... I have come that they may have life, and have it to the full. (v 10)

A modern approach to finding inner strength is to gain a sense of security by surrounding yourself with material possessions. One man I know has a home filled with precious antiques, but he can hardly sleep at night for someone might break in and carry off his treasures! People with inner strength are not always secure financially.

Many people today are turning to transcendental meditation in their search for inner calm. There is no doubt meditation techniques do have a pacifying effect. However, true peace – the peace that comes from God – can be found only through a personal relationship with Jesus Christ.

The term 'self-expression' is frequently used by modern men and women. People attempt to find inner strength through self-knowledge and self-cultivation. Self-knowledge is fine if it is linked to God, but when it is linked only to the self then it will result in self-deterioration. Cultivate self without God and it disintegrates; cultivate it with God and it will develop.

🖋 *Gracious Father, outside of You there is nothing but death; with You there is nothing but life. Thank You my Father. In Jesus' Name. Amen.*

JESUS DEMONSTRATED POISE

FOR READING & MEDITATION – JOHN 6:1–15

Jesus, knowing that they intended to come and make him
king by force, withdrew again to a mountain by himself. (v 15)

No one, of course, has had greater inner strength and spiritual poise than our Lord Jesus Christ. As a youth He was unperturbed when his parents chastised Him for getting lost. A far more severe test of his inner strength came when He was led by the Spirit into the desert to be tempted by the devil. His forty days of fasting there were enough to leave him exhausted. Yet the account says: 'He returned ... in the power of the Spirit' (Luke 4:14).

Jesus had inner strength not only when his life was being threatened but in times of adulation also. Today we read that the crowd wanted to make Him king, but Jesus 'withdrew again to a mountain by himself'. He withdrew to pray and be alone with God. He would not allow Himself to be swept off his feet by people's adulation. Opposition could not break Him nor success unsteady Him. He was inwardly proof against both.

O Father, give me the inner strength to handle anything that comes my way – both failure and success. In Jesus' Name I pray. Amen.

AN UNSHAKABLE KINGDOM

FOR READING & MEDITATION – HEBREWS 12:14–29

Therefore, since we are receiving a kingdom that
cannot be shaken, let us be thankful … (v 28)

As I reflected on the elements that contribute to my own inner
strength – an astonishing calmness that sometimes surprises me
– I discovered seven principles which I know will work for you.

The first principle is the one found in our text for today: recognising that we belong to an unshakable kingdom.

This text is one of the most steadying in the New Testament. All
around us men and women are attempting to build on the basis of
power, pride, position, and learning, but these are shakable. Throughout time, empires have been built on earthly values and ideologies
alone – ideologies that were meant to last for a thousand years.

Where are these empires now? Gone, for they were built on shakable foundations. In the years that lie ahead we will witness many
earthly kingdoms shaking and falling before our eyes. I don't know
about you, but to me it means everything to know there is one unshakable kingdom.

*Heavenly Father, what comfort it gives to know that my feet
are established in an unshakable kingdom. For that I am deeply
grateful. In Jesus' Name. Amen.*

RECEIVING THE KINGDOM

FOR READING & MEDITATION – JOHN 18:28–40

Jesus said, 'My kingdom is not of this world.' (v 36)

Jesus Christ is the King of an unshakable kingdom, the only un-shaken power in a shaking world.

How can one become part of this unshakable kingdom? The good news is that we don't have to strive to become part of Christ's king-dom – we simply have to receive it.

For many people, receiving Christ is not easy. They want to earn their passage to heaven or do something to be saved. But the gospel of Jesus Christ, put simply, comes down to this: you have to remove the barriers of pride in your heart, recognise that you can do nothing to save yourself, and receive Him into your life by an act of faith. You say to Jesus Christ, 'Come into my life and have your say.' When you do that, then you are possessed by the kingdom and the kingdom possesses you. Have you taken that step? If not, open your life to Jesus Christ I beg you, and receive Him now.

O God, I let go of my unsurrendered self. Come into my life, forgive my sins, and reign in every part of my life. In Jesus' Name. Amen.

'JAPANESE LANTERNS'

FOR READING & MEDITATION – ROMANS 10:1–13

… if you confess with your mouth, 'Jesus is Lord,' and believe in your heart that God raised him from the dead, you will be saved. (v 9)

An evangelist tells of holding a Christian meeting in an out-of-the-way village in Japan. As he approached the church in the darkness he saw men standing at the various intersections holding lighted Japanese lanterns on which the shape of a cross was visible. These men were directing people to the church, encouraging them by means of the illuminated crosses to turn in and hear the Word of life.

You see, a personal encounter with the Jesus of the cross, is the only way by which men and women can enter God's kingdom. God says: 'I will meet anyone, no matter what sins they have committed, but I will only meet them at the cross.'

When you come by faith to the cross – the place where Christ died for you – and receive him into your life as your Saviour then you will find your feet firmly planted on the solid foundations of a kingdom that can never be shaken.

O God, I bow before your cross in repentance and surrender. Establish me in your unshakable kingdom. Amen.

FROM STRENGTH TO WEAKNESS

For reading & meditation – Acts 2:14–28

I saw the Lord always before me. Because he
is at my right hand, I will not be shaken. (v 25)

Notice that for all those who have accepted Christ as their Saviour this Lord of an unshakable kingdom is not only before us but beside us – 'at my right hand'.

If we knew that He would be with us in the future, but was not with us in the present, then we would be shakable. However, He holds the present as well as the future. The right hand is usually equated with strength. For the Lord to be at my right hand is for him to be at my strongest point.

We are inclined to think that the Lord comes to our weak point to strengthen us. Although that is true, it is also true that He is at our strong point to save it from turning into weakness. One Christian writer says: 'Our weakness gets us into trouble, but our strength gets us into trouble even more.' How true. So easily the light in us can turn to darkness.

O God, I recognise that I need You not only at my weak point but also at my strong point. Help me my Father. In Jesus' Name. Amen.

PETER'S POINT OF FAILURE

For reading & meditation – Luke 22:54–62

Peter replied, 'Man, I don't know what you're talking about!' Just as he was speaking, the cock crowed. (v 60)

The Bible contains many examples of people who failed not only at the point of their weakness but also at the point of their strengths. It was said of Moses that he was the meekest man on the earth (Num 12:3 KJV). But he allowed anger to override his meekness and disobeyed God.

Simon Peter also failed at this point. His strength, his 'right hand', loyalty and commitment, became his weakness. Peter's pride went before his fall with his denial of Jesus. He needed the Lord at his right hand to strengthen the qualities of loyalty and commitment with humility.

Those who are involved in Christian work sometimes become so anxious to see their work succeed that they exaggerate the success out of the very desire to see it, and border on the untruthful. They need the Lord to be at their right hand in order to ensure their deepest longings are combined with honesty, realism, and an acceptance of the facts.

Father, help me set a watch not only where I am weak but also where I am strong. In Jesus' Name. Amen.

THE NATURE OF REALITY

FOR READING & MEDITATION – 2 CORINTHIANS 2:12–17

But thanks be to God, who always leads us
in triumphal procession in Christ … (v 14)

A well known theologian said, 'Whilst the resurrection of Jesus was the result of God's power bringing Him back to life, it was also based on the nature of reality.' Although the resurrection of Jesus was effected by a specific act of God, there is a sense in which it resulted also from an intrinsic fact, namely that it was possible for him to die, but not possible for him to be held captive by it. He had to rise, being who He was.

We cannot be shaken because in Christ we are in reality with a capital 'R'. We can rise above every circumstance, overcome all obstacles, because we belong to a kingdom that simply cannot be shaken. It would be easier to put the Atlantic ocean into a thimble, than shake the kingdom which has Christ as its King.

We can rise above every circumstance – even death, for death is a circumstance, not an inner-stance. In Christ, death has died, not Him.

O God, I am awed at the wonder of your perfect protection and preservation. What can life or death do to me? Amen.

'STILL IN THE PENCIL'

<small>FOR READING & MEDITATION – PHILIPPIANS 3:1–11</small>

Finally, my brothers, rejoice in the Lord! (v 1)

Are you someone whose heart is glad? If your heart is resting on God then it follows that you will have a glad heart.

But in addition to the glad or joyful heart we must have a tongue that rejoices. 'My heart is glad and my tongue rejoices.' If there is no expression the time will come when there is nothing to express. The tongue must express itself both in praise to God and sharing with others the goodness of God.

When others look at us, what impression do they get? Gloom or gladness, sadness or serenity? A little girl was asked by her teacher where the dot was that should have been over the letter 'I' in her essay. 'Oh, that's still in the pencil,' she said. Whenever God gives you a blessing, pass it on. Billy Graham says: 'If God can't get out then maybe He won't come in.' Inflow and outflow – that's the heartbeat of the Christian life.

<small>*Staying spiritually strong*</small>

<small>NOVEMBER 12</small>

🖎 *O God, help me to have a heart from which gladness overflows and lips to praise You and tell others of your goodness. In Jesus' Name. Amen.*

'GIVE ME A JOB'

FOR READING & MEDITATION – PSALM 45:1–17

My heart is stirred by a noble theme as I recite my verses
for the king; my tongue is the pen of a skilful writer. (v 1)

Acts 2:26 reads: 'Therefore my heart is glad and my tongue rejoices.' Another verse says: 'For out of the abundance of the
heart the mouth speaks' (Matt 12:34 NKJV). I do not want to add to
Scripture, yet I think it is true to say that if the mouth doesn't
speak then there will be little or no abundance to speak of. No one
can maintain their divinely-given inner strength unless they share
what they are being given.

However, outflow is not to be directed only to the unconverted;
it must be directed to fellow Christians also. When Christians
meet, whether in the high street or in the home, their conversation should include the Lord. How sad that so often when Christians get together they talk about everything but the Lord. As you
move out into the world today, share something of the Lord with
others, whether they be Christians or non-Christians. The more
you give out the more will come in.

Staying spiritually strong

❧ *Dear Lord, give me a glad heart and a rejoicing tongue. Enable me to show a joyful face. In Jesus' Name I pray. Amen.*

NOVEMBER 13

REVERENT LISTENING

FOR READING & MEDITATION – MATTHEW 6:1–15

But when you pray, go into your room, close the door
and pray to your Father, who is unseen. (v 6)

If we are to be men and women with inner spiritual strength we
need to cultivate a daily Quiet Time. Those who say they can live
in a state of prayer without definite times of prayer will probably
find themselves without both. They are as foolish as those who
say they can live in a state of physical nourishment without stated
times for meals.

The daily Quiet Time is an 'idleness' that results in renewed
activity. You become alive all over. The great French philosopher
Blaise Pascal concluded: 'Nearly all the ills of life spring from this
simple source that we are not able to sit still in a room.'

But what if in that stillness we met with God – how healing
that would be. James Russell Lowell wrote:

If the chosen soul could never be alone
In deep mid-silence, open-doored to God,
No greatness ever had been dreamed or done ...
The nurse of full-grown souls is solitude.

O God, help me see even more clearly the importance of the
daily Quiet Time. Amen.

A HIGHER LEVEL

FOR READING & MEDITATION – PSALM 5:1–12

In the morning, O LORD, you hear my voice; in the morning
I lay my requests before you and wait in expectation. (v 3)

A traveller tells of his experience the first time he passed
through the Panama Canal. 'We felt a lifting, great fountains
were opened from beneath, and to our astonishment that great
ship was lifted thirty-five feet in just seven minutes. Then the gates
opened and we glided out on a higher level.' The effect of the
Quiet Time can be likened to that experience: it shuts you in with
God, the door closes upon you, and you may at first feel helpless,
so shut in, so inactive. And then infinite resources begin to bubble
up from beneath, and you are lifted, without any noise or strain,
to a more elevated level.

It is best to have your Quiet Time in the first hours of the morning. If it is not possible to set aside time in the morning then take
any hour you can. But resolve that no day will go by without attempting to spend time with God.

*O God my Father, help me gaze at You before my eyes meet the
gaze of the world. In Jesus' Name. Amen.*

SPIRITUAL TOUCH

For reading & meditation – Luke 8:40–56

She came up behind him and touched the edge of his cloak,
and immediately her bleeding stopped. (v 44)

One preacher has warned, 'Those who do not provide for a
Quiet Time in the morning may have to provide for unquiet
time throughout the day.'

God has infinite resources not only for the asking but also for the
taking. During the Quiet Time the soul grows more receptive and
'becomes the organ of spiritual touch' – that touch becoming as
rewarding as that of the woman in our story today as she reached
out and touched the edge of Christ's cloak.

In the Quiet Time we exchange our impotence for his power,
our unrest for his rest, our grief for his joy. The Quiet Time produces a quiet heart which becomes a quiet confidence and a quiet
power. It is then that the soul becomes its best. It is then that you
tune in to God's wavelength.

As often as possible, begin the day with God. Let this be your
motto: Without You not one step over the threshold. With You –
anywhere.

*O God, resources are so near at hand. May I take the time that
is necessary to avail myself of them. In Jesus' Name. Amen.*

'DON'T LEAVE HOME WITHOUT IT'

FOR READING & MEDITATION – LUKE 9:18–27

Once when Jesus was praying in private and his disciples were
with him, he asked them, 'Who do the crowds say I am?' (v 1)

When the charismatic renewal was beginning to hit a large
number of churches, many people began to develop a different attitude to the daily Quiet Time. Some argued, 'Now I am
baptised in the Spirit I no longer need my daily Quiet Time. I have
a perpetual "Quiet Time" – a moment-by-moment contact with
God that extends through all my waking hours.' I pointed out that
if Jesus needed to have stated times of quiet to be alone with God
then we do far more.

The daily Quiet Time is not a demand that God makes; it is a
discipline that fortifies and enriches life.

The benefit of having a Quiet Time first thing in the morning is
that if we go out into the day with a God-reference rather than a
self-reference then we are more likely to have an island of quiet
within whatever pressures we face. The Quiet Time produces a
quietness that becomes the atmosphere for the day.

*O God, give me the sense to guard the times of communion I
have with You so that I develop inner strength. Amen.*

LIVING OFF THE SURFACE

FOR READING & MEDITATION – JEREMIAH 17:1–10

... blessed is the man who trusts in the LORD ... He will be like a tree planted by the water that sends out its roots by the stream. (vv 7–8)

Billy Graham has said: 'If you are too busy to spend a little time with God each day in personal prayer and the reading of his Word, then you are busier than God intends you to be.'

It is preferable to set aside time in the morning, but before we move on I would like to share this thought which I came across in my reading. 'A diver too busy to think about getting his line for air in working order before he descends to the depths would be no more foolish than the man or woman who descends into the stifling atmosphere of today's world without getting their breathing apparatus of prayer connected with the pure air of the kingdom of God above.' One reason why so many Christians are spiritually anaemic is because they have done themselves the harm of self-inflicted asphyxiation.

Ask yourself now: Am I a stunted spiritual being? You will be if you do not regularly meet with God.

O God, You who sent your Son to give us life in all its fullness, help me send my tap root down into your resources. Amen.

GOD'S OBLIGATION

FOR READING & MEDITATION – ISAIAH 55:1–13

... so is my word that goes out from my mouth. It will not return
to me empty, but will accomplish what I desire ... (v 11)

In the Quiet Time what should we do? When I studied the lives of
men and women – both living and dead – noted for their devotional lives, several features became apparent.

George Muller, a man who had a rich devotional life and who
founded the famous orphanage in Bristol, England, said, 'I have a
prayer list with me and begin to pray for needs.' 'Try starting your
Quiet Time by opening up the Scriptures,' his friend suggested,
'and see what happens.' George Muller followed this advice and
later admitted: '... it changed the whole atmosphere of my Quiet
Time and brought a richness into it.'

The reading of Scripture primes your spiritual pump, so to
speak, and moves the soul in the direction of God. The Lord has
promised, as our text for today assures us, to bless his own Word.
It is important to remember that all comments are secondary, and
not a substitute for first-hand contact with the Word of God.

🕊 *O God, help me saturate my inner being with your mind. In
Jesus' Name. Amen.*

SPEAK LORD ...

FOR READING & MEDITATION – PSALM 119:105–112

Your statutes are my heritage for ever;

they are the joy of my heart. (v 111)

A good suggestion to follow in our Quiet Time is to pause for a little while after prayerful contemplation of the Scriptures to see if God will say anything to you. Be silent before God.

When you become receptive, then you will soon find that God will come close to you to guide, direct, and develop your spirituality. He will take advantage of your receptivity to make you the best you can be.

It is always helpful to have a notebook and pen with you during your Quiet Time so that you can record anything that strikes you or anything that God may say to you. The notebook and pen are a sign of faith since they show that you expect some message to come to you. Once you have read the Word you will find your thinking and aspirations start moving in the right direction. And you will pray prayers that are in harmony with the will of God.

Staying spiritually strong

NOVEMBER 20

🕊 *O God, amid all the hustle and bustle of life help me to be silent. In Christ's Name I pray. Amen.*

THE POWER OF PAUSE

For reading & meditation – Psalm 37:1–17

Be still before the LORD and wait patiently for him … (v 7)

The suggestions made so far regarding our Quiet Time have been these: spend some time reading God's Word. After reading, stay relaxed and receptive and ask God, 'Father, have You anything to say to me?' Learn to listen. Write down any message that comes. If you do not write down the inspiration or word of guidance it may fade as you go out and become immersed in the business of the day.

The final part of your Quiet Time should be taken up with the things that you want to say to God. Express your adoration of God. Always start there.

Remember, too, that prayer is not a monologue but a dialogue, so be alert for anything the Lord may say to you concerning your petitions.

Build pauses into your petitions. Pause to see if God wants to speak to you. People who walk through life with 'something inside so strong' are people, I assure you, who have cultivated quiet moments with God.

Father, please help me to have the resources that will enable me to stand tall and strong in the midst of today's world. Amen.

WHEN THINGS GO WRONG

FOR READING & MEDITATION – 2 CHRONICLES 7:1–10

... they worshipped and gave thanks to the LORD, saying,
'He is good; his love endures for ever.' (v 3)

Another element that contributes to inner spiritual strength and poise is a firm belief in the goodness of God. No soul can experience deep inner peace unless it rests ultimately in the goodness of God.

If I were to live for a thousand years I doubt if I could say anything more important than that. If you go through life harbouring doubts about the goodness of God then your inner strength and poise will quickly be sabotaged. Happiness, it has been said, depends on things happening happily. But what about when things don't happen happily? Can we still believe that God is good?

We come to a critical issue here, for if we believe that God is good only when things go our way, then when things don't go our way, or God doesn't give us the answer to our prayers which we desire, we will quickly lose our peace and poise. And what good is a poise that depends on circumstances?

Father, help me drop my anchor into the reassuring and encouraging depths of the revelation that You are good. In Jesus' Name. Amen.

WHEN SATAN TALKS THEOLOGY

FOR READING & MEDITATION – GENESIS 3:1–19

'You will not surely die,' the serpent said to the woman. (v 4)

The aim of the very first temptation was to impugn the character of God and suggest that He is not good. When Satan, in the form of a serpent, entered the garden in order to tempt Eve he talked theology. The devil knew it was impossible to cast doubt on the existence of God so he attempted to cast doubt on the goodness of God. His purpose was to put into Eve's mind the thought that if God loved her then He would not have prevented her eating fruit from the tree (2:17).

To believe in the goodness of God when your life has been turned upside down is not easy, but unless we find a way of being convinced of that truth we will not experience the inner strength that is necessary for us to stand up to this world. There can never be deep inner peace and harmony in the soul unless it rests ultimately in the goodness of God.

My Father and my God, help me develop a deep conviction which will keep me buttressed. This I pray in Jesus' Name. Amen.

ALL IS WELL

For reading & meditation – Psalm 34:1–22

Taste and see that the LORD is good; blessed is
the man who takes refuge in him. (v 8)

Because of a fuel shortage some people attending meetings in Nigeria had to set out several hours in advance in order to arrive at a meeting on time. Yet in the services I found the Christians calm and composed and ready to laugh. They packed the building in which I was speaking, and at almost every meeting a leader would stand and call out, 'God is good.' The congregation would respond with these words, 'All the time.' This procedure would then be repeated, affirming once again, 'God is good.' One well-known hymn they sang brought tears to my eyes:

When peace, like a river, attendeth my way,
When sorrows, like sea-billows, roll,
Whatever my lot, Thou hast taught me to say,
It is well, it is well with my soul.

When I asked one Nigerian lady how she remained calm, poised, and cheerful under such circumstances, she responded, 'I don't live under the circumstances, I live over them. I live in God.'

Father, help me live over my circumstances, not under them. Give me the faith that looks at a Person – your Son Jesus Christ. Amen.

'IF NOT' FAITH

For reading & meditation – Daniel 3:1–30

I see four men walking around in the fire ...
and the fourth looks like a son of the gods. (v 25)

If God is good then why does He not deliver us from the tribulations we sometimes have to face? Why does He not respond to our requests for his help in escaping from overwhelming sorrows and difficulties? Love and goodness may deny the thing asked for only because there is a wiser and bigger purpose.

Never let your faith depend on a particular thing happening. It is not wrong to hope for it, to long for it, even to pray for it. If you do rest your faith on a particular happening then your faith will increase or decrease according to whether or not that happening takes place. But if your faith is in God and his goodness then it will remain constant whether what you long for happens or not.

The faith that says, 'I believe God,' is good. Better by far, however, is the faith that says: 'But even if He does not do it, I will still believe He is good.'

Help me, my Father, to trust your goodness even when I cannot trace it. I rest not in the immediate but in the Ultimate – in You. Amen.

A LOVING HAND ON THE HELM

FOR READING & MEDITATION – ISAIAH 30:1–18

… in quietness and trust is your strength … (v 15)

Sometimes God denies us a shallow answer so that we may put our roots deeper into eternal reality, and consequently stand tall and strong in any future storm.

A Welsh preacher used to say, 'We must learn to live in time and eternity simultaneously.' If the time side of life seems to be full of trouble then the eternity side holds us steady.

A missionary to the Chinese people was asked for the secret of his poise and inner strength. He answered, 'Confidence in the goodness of God.' Pressed to expand on that statement, he added, 'I have come to the place in my Christian life where I am convinced that in the midst of the worst thing that can happen there is a good and wise purpose at work. Thus I can go on, knowing that love is at the helm of my life. God loves me too much to let anything happen to me that will not work out for good.'

Father, I too rest in the Ultimate, not in the immediate. In You I am impregnable. I trust You and rejoice in your goodness. In Jesus' Name. Amen.

MADE FOR WORSHIP

FOR READING & MEDITATION – JOB 1:6–22

At this, Job got up and tore his robe and shaved his
head. Then he fell to the ground in worship … (v 20)

To believe that God is good is easy when the sun is shining and
everything is going well, but what about when God allows a
tragedy to overtake you? Can you then say with deep conviction,
'Yes, God is good'? Many Christians still utter the words, but without
conviction.

In our passage today Job is presented to us as a fabulously
wealthy and successful man, the father of a large and happy family.
Then all at once, like a bolt out of the blue, tidings of disaster
come crashing in upon him. Hot on the heels of one another come
the messengers of woe. The reports are desolating. His oxen and
donkeys are gone, his sheep and camels are gone, his servants are
gone, his sons and daughters are gone. With a single stroke he is
bereft of almost everything. But Job, hearing the numbing news,
falls down on the ground and *worships*.

For worship is what we were made for.

O Father, if I have any doubts that interfere with my worship
of You then show me how they can be dissolved. Amen.

NO APOLOGIES

FOR READING & MEDITATION – PSALM 86:1–17

You are forgiving and good, O LORD, abounding
in love to all who call to you. (v 5)

Yesterday we admitted it is not easy to believe in the goodness
of God when tragedy strikes. As Christians we are taught in
Scripture not only that God is good, but that He is all powerful
also. The presence of sin in his universe has not blunted his
power one iota. What He was He is, and what He is He was, and
what He is and was He ever will be – all powerful, all knowing,
and ever present. Christians are called to take God on trust, to
believe that He allows bad things to happen not because He is
powerless to prevent them but because a sovereign purpose is at
work that we, in our present state, cannot comprehend.

Nowhere in the Bible does God ever apologise for allowing what
we call tragedies or disasters to occur. Instead, He asks us to trust
Him, to believe that 'in all things God works for the good of those
who love him' (Rom 8:28).

*O Father, help me, dear Father, to believe in your goodness
even when seemingly bad things happen in my life. Amen.*

THE ONE SAFE PLACE

FOR READING & MEDITATION – PSALM 106:1–12

Give thanks to the LORD, for he is good;
his love endures for ever. (v 1)

How do we go about building confidence in a God who allows bad things to happen to good people, and to do it in a way that is in complete accord with Scripture? I know of only one way – to gaze upon the cross. Theologians throughout the ages have asserted that the cross is the one fixed point in the universe where God's character is made clear.

A God who gave his Son to die for me on Calvary just has to be good. That is where I stand whenever I am tempted to question God's goodness – I stand at the cross. So have countless others who have gone through personal afflictions. There the matter of God's goodness has been validated for all time, and in the light that comes from the cross I am able to make my way in the darkness. Those who would enjoy 'something inside so strong' must have a deep conviction that God is good.

My Father and my God, help me to take my stand at the foot of the cross for there, in its light, I see light. In Jesus' Name. Amen.

DEFEATING OUR ENEMIES

FOR READING & MEDITATION – HEBREWS 12:1–13

My son, do not make light of the Lord's discipline,
and do not lose heart when he rebukes you ...(v 5)

Those who walk through life with 'something inside so strong' are people also who know how to eliminate from their lives those things that dissipate their inner strength. This is why the principle on which we are now about to focus should be regarded as one of the most important. The principle is this: defeat your soul's enemies.

The first of these is *lingering resentment*. I use the word 'lingering' because resentment can arise in our hearts almost without us realising it. Once we are aware of it, however, we must not, we dare not, allow it to remain. A certain missionary was returned from the mission field on the verge of a nervous breakdown. During counselling he confessed to harbouring resentment against a fellow missionary. He gave up his resentment and returned to the field a new man.

The answer to resentment is forgiveness. Don't ever say you can't forgive. Grace is available to help you do so.

O God, I forgive all who have hurt me, and open myself to your grace. In Jesus' Name. Amen.

'I AM NOT AFRAID OF YOU'

FOR READING & MEDITATION – ISAIAH 41:1–14

'So do not fear, for I am with you; do not
be dismayed, for I am your God.' (v 10)

*F*ear is an enemy of the soul which dissipates our inner spiritual strength. However, there is a fear that brings wisdom, and a fear that makes one bury the talents that have been given by God. It is the unhealthy fear that must be rooted out at all costs.

First, admit your fear with open-eyed honesty. Don't pretend it is not there. Second, be sure you want to really get rid of your fear. Often fear produces physical illnesses that in turn determine our life strategy. So will to be free.

Third, remember every fear you feel has been defeated by Christ. You need not be defeated by anything unless you consent to be. Fourth, surrender your fear into the hands of God. Turn it right over to God and ask Him to deliver you from it. Fear results from keeping things in your own hands; faith is placing them in the hands of God – and leaving them there.

O Father, I turn my fears over into your competent hands. I do so now. I accept my release with gratitude. I am free. Amen.

Staying spiritually strong

DECEMBER 1

FALSE AND REAL GUILT

<small>FOR READING & MEDITATION – 1 JOHN 1:1–10</small>

If we confess our sins, he is faithful and just
and will forgive us our sins ... (v 9)

Another enemy of inner strength and security is *unresolved guilt*. We cannot live with guilt, that is, truly live.

Guilt – real guilt – that results from having broken one of God's laws must be dissolved through repentance and prayer, and be washed in the blood of Christ. A sense of real guilt is heavy to carry and weighs down the soul, but actually it is a mercy. Just think what condition our souls would be in if, after we had violated one of God's principles, we felt no guilt. Some, of course, have learned to cauterise their conscience so that they feel no guilt. But Christians who regularly meet with God will not do that.

The way to deal with guilt is quite simple: identify the violation and ask God to forgive it. If restitution is required or you need to ask someone to forgive you then do what is necessary. Dissolve all guilt in the blood of Christ. It cannot live there.

<small>DECEMBER 2 | *Staying spiritually strong*</small>

🌱 *Father, whenever guilt descends upon my soul, help me come to You at once to gain cleansing and forgiveness. In Jesus' Name. Amen.*

TEARS DID IT

FOR READING & MEDITATION – 2 CORINTHIANS 5:11–21

And he died for all, that those who live should no longer
live for themselves but for him who died for them ... (v 15)

Our verse identifies another enemy of spiritual strength and poise: *self-centredness*.

'There is a fundamental law of life written into the constitution of things, and more people get broken by this law than by any other single thing in life,' writes one theologian. What is that law? Concentrate on yourself and you will lose yourself. Concentrate on what you can do for others and how you can give yourself to them and you will find yourself.

While talking to a small group of women a competent public speaker broke down and wept. Subsequently she wrote to each one who had witnessed this event and asked them not to mention her tears. In time, however, she came to see that the breakdown of herself was the best thing that could have happened to her. It led her to offer herself in a new way to God. Instead of concentrating on herself and her reputation she placed herself in God's hands. Tears did it.

🐾 *God, lead me away from my petty self to your plentiful self. Help me walk through that door which leads to You. In Jesus' Name. Amen.*

Staying spiritually strong

DECEMBER 3

SEVER WITH SELF

FOR READING & MEDITATION – PHILIPPIANS 3:12–21

Forgetting what is behind and straining towards what
is ahead, I press on towards the goal … (vv 13–14)

We continue identifying the enemies that diminish our spiritual power. Now we come to the fifth of these enemies:
undisciplined desires. Desires are the God-given forces of the
personality. Without desire we would vegetate. Buddha tried to
encourage people to gain victory over their desires by cutting the
root of desire itself. This would enable mankind to become desire-
less and go out into what is called *nirvana.* But getting rid of
desire because it causes problems is like cutting off your head because you have a headache.

Our desires must be brought under control. Find a person who
goes through life with spiritual poise and power and you will find
someone who has learned how to discipline their desires.

The secret of spiritual discipline is: love for Jesus Christ. The
more in love with Him you are the easier self-discipline becomes.
It then becomes a matter not so much of trying but trusting –
trusting Him to work in you and through you.

*O God, my desires need to be mastered by a Person who is
stronger than I. Be my Master I pray. Amen.*

NON-CONFORMITY

FOR READING & MEDITATION – EPHESIANS 2:1–10

... you followed the ways of this world and of the ruler
of the kingdom of the air, the spirit who is now
at work in those who are disobedient. (v 2)

Conformity is the sixth enemy. Note these words: 'Society demands conformity; if you fall beneath its standards it will
punish you; if you rise above its standards it will persecute you. It
demands a grey average conformity.' This is why even Christians
succumb and become echoes instead of voices. However, this retreat into anonymity will not characterise those who know how
to avail themselves of the inner strength which Christ provides.

A certain man admitted: 'Prior to my conversion I would never
stick my neck out, never stand up and be counted.' At a meeting
of residents the man stood up and spoke against the evils of ra-
cism after which most of the residents burst out in prolonged applause. Under the sway of the prevailing philosophy of life they
themselves didn't dare dissent.

Many are afflicted with this creeping moral paralysis. They look
around, not up, before they act. Conform to the things that are
right, but where there are wrongs, be a non-conformist.

O God, help me be more like Jesus. For His Name's sake. Amen.

'THERE'S ROOM AT THIS INN'

FOR READING & MEDITATION – JAMES 3:1–18

Out of the same mouth come praise and cursing.
My brothers, this should not be. (v 10)

Another enemy that threatens spiritual strength and poise is this: *mixed motives.*

Let's think of our own behaviour. Do we who preach the gospel do so for self-display or for the approving word at the end of the sermon rather than the approval of God? Are we afraid to offend a rich contributor but not afraid to offend our own moral nature? People who possess inner spiritual strength and poise will not be perfect, but they continually check their motives to ensure they are not mixed.

Mixed motives must be banished as far as is possible. When next you are having your time of prayer relax with all your defences down. Say to God, 'If there are any mixed motives in me then please bring them to the surface.' If you become aware of some, confess them and ask God to purge them from your soul. Get rid of all mixed motives. They are germs which will make your soul sick.

🖙 *Father, I am blind to my own weaknesses. Help me to be honest with myself. In Jesus' Name. Amen.*

'DON'T YOU UNDERSTAND?'

FOR READING & MEDITATION – 2 TIMOTHY 2:1–19
Do your best to present yourself to God as one approved,
a workman ... who correctly handles the word of truth. (v 15)

Now we consider the last of the eight enemies that can diminish our spiritual strength: *ignorance and lack of judgement.*

The Christian outlook is, 'The truth will set you free'. Spiritually strong Christians are those who seek to develop their understanding, first by reading Scripture and then good literature. Our conscience works within the framework of sound information and knowledge. For the safest and best judgements, our minds must be Christianly informed and trained.

Follow these steps: (1) Go over your life and see where you may be ignorant. (2) Acquaint yourself with the great social issues of the day and the principles of Scripture that relate to them. (3) Read one good book a week. If you take a speed-reading course you will be able to read three a week. (4) Review your judgements and don't be afraid to reverse them. You will be more careful in making up your mind if deep down your mind knows all judgements will be reviewed.

☙ *My Father and my God, I would have an informed mind for I am in the serious business of being my best for You. In Jesus' Name. Amen.*

GIVE THANKS

For reading & meditation – Matthew 15:29–39
Then he took the seven loaves and the fish, and when he had given
thanks, he broke them and gave them to the disciples … (v 36)

Another characteristic of those who possess a deep inner spiritual strength is a thankful heart. 'So far as thanksgiving is
concerned,' said Dr WE Sangster, 'the mass of people can be divided
into two classes: those who take things for granted, and those who
take things with gratitude.' I wonder to which class you belong.

Sir John Templeton, a financier and a philanthropist, believes
that until you can recognise the good things that are going on
around you, you do not have a proper basis for handling life.

Before our Lord took the loaves and fish and handed them to
the disciples He gave thanks. Jesus made it a practice to thank God
for his goodness in all things. He was constantly giving thanks.
And so must we. Someone has said, 'The most foolish person in
the world is that person who complains about what he does not
have instead of being thankful for what he does have.' How true.

☙ My Father and my God, help me cultivate a thankful and
praising heart; teach me how to count my blessings. In Jesus'
Name. Amen.

COUNT YOUR BLESSINGS

For reading & meditation – Psalm 147:1–20

Sing to the Lord with thanksgiving;
make music to our God on the harp. (v 7)

Sir John Templeton says for every single problem we will find ten blessings if we look for them. Human nature, however, is more drawn to bad news.

I talked to a Christian man who was obviously blessed with an inner spiritual poise, and I put to him the idea that one of the characteristics of spiritually secure people is that they have a thankful and praising heart. 'I have never thought of it before,' he said, 'but hardly an hour goes by without my heart rising in praise and gratitude to God for something or other.' 'What things?' I asked. After pausing briefly he said, 'Things like the fertile earth, my five senses, a measure of health, an unimpaired reason, the love of my family, the song of the birds, the laughter of children ...' On and on he went. Do you thank God for the common blessings which can so easily be overlooked? Don't wait until you lose them to be grateful.

O God, help me develop keen sight so that I do not miss one of the multiplicity of your benefits to me. Give me a thankful heart. Amen.

DON'T MISS THE MERCIES

FOR READING & MEDITATION – COLOSSIANS 3:1–17

Let the peace of Christ rule in your hearts … And be thankful. (v 5)

Most of us enjoy the blessing of unimpaired reason. Do we thank God for that? Look around you today. Think of such things as the wonder of the universe, the fact that the sun rises and sets with mathematical precision, that the stars stay in their courses, and so on. Think more about the good than the bad.

It is not always easy, of course, to give thanks. How can you thank God for cancer, for example? As one who has experienced a battle with this disease, I can say that though one cannot thank God for cancer, there are many mercies surrounding it for which one can be thankful: the fact that God does not desert us at times of illness, the tenderness and concern of those who give medical attention, the love and encouragement of others, and so on.

There are mercies to be found at the heart of tragedies. Look for the mercies and be thankful for them.

O Father, I will start today to count not the bad things but the blessings. In Jesus' Name. Amen.

'WHEN DID I EVER FAIL THEE?'

FOR READING & MEDITATION – PSALM 103:1–22

Praise the LORD, O my soul, and forget not all his benefits ... (v 2)

St Teresa of Avila was depressed one day. She forgot the many deliverances and blessings that God had given her. In the midst of her darkness the Lord came to her and said: 'When did I ever fail thee? I am today what I have always been.' Her depression quickly lifted and her heart was once again filled with praise.

How sad that we forget so easily the blessings of God. That is why new dangers startle us and cause fear and uncertainty – we have forgotten past mercies. We would be calm and confident in present trouble if we remembered vividly the deliverances that have already taken place. We would say to ourselves, 'The God who delivered me then will not desert me now.' John Newton, the one-time slave trader who became a preacher and hymn writer, was assured of this:

His love in time past forbids me to think
He'll leave me at last in trouble to sink.

🐦 *Father, forgive me that I am fearful in the midst of trouble. I have a loving Father in heaven. Help me to remember that. Amen.*

WATCH THE DIFFERENCE

For reading & meditation – James 1:1–18

Every good and perfect gift is … from the Father of the
heavenly lights, who does not change like shifting shadows. (v 17)

Why is it *good* to give thanks unto the Lord, as the psalmist
says? First, it cultivates an awareness that we maintain our
existence on this earth by the Almighty's favour. Second, it helps
us conserve the concept of reverence without which every mortal
mind is deficient.

Third, it preserves a sense of happiness and goodwill. Anyone
who has developed a spirit of thankfulness will face life buoyantly
and confidently because they are conscious of the mercies that
flow from heaven. The great preacher Charles Haddon Spurgeon
said this: 'It is a delightful and profitable occupation to mark the
hand of God in the lives of his ancient saints and to observe his
goodness in delivering them, *but would it not be more interesting and profitable for us to notice the hand of God in our own
lives?*' (emphasis mine).

Start every day by thinking of five things for which you can be
thankful – and watch the difference in your days.

*O God, help me start every day with thanksgiving. For your
own dear Name's sake I pray.*

GIVING BACK TO GOD

For reading & meditation – 2 Samuel 23:8–17

> But he refused to drink it; instead,
> he poured it out before the LORD. (v 16)

David looked out across the valley towards Bethlehem, the town where he grew up. He thought of the well at which he had often drunk. 'Oh, that someone would get me a drink of water from the well near the gate of Bethlehem!' he cried (v 15). Quick as a flash three of his trusted men – 'mighty men' says Scripture – raced through the Philistine lines to the well, scooped up a flask of its clear water, and returned safely to David's side. Stunned and amazed by their devotion and their costly gift, David accepted it, then poured it out on the ground in thanksgiving to God.

How did the three mighty men react to this? They would have understood that David's action was triggered not by a lack of appreciation but out of a deep desire to give something that was so precious to him back to God.

Will you give thanks to God for his gifts of love for you today?

Father, help me not to miss one single thing that I might offer back to You in thanksgiving, praise and adoration. In Jesus' Name. Amen.

NO OCCASION TO
BE THANKFUL?

FOR READING & MEDITATION – PSALM 100:1–5

Enter his gates with thanksgiving and his courts with praise ... (v 4)

How blind can people be! Even belief in the fall of man does not save one from amazement and shame at the myopic view many people have of the world around them. If we pause and reflect, we will find numerous causes for thankfulness – small things as well as large ones.

I have come to the conclusion that one of the reasons why people can't thank God for the special blessings of life is because they fail to see Him in the common blessings of life – the gentle warmth of the sun, the first cry of a baby, the wonderful variety of fruits, vegetables and flowers from the earth, and so on.

Miss out on the common things and you are likely to miss out on the bigger things. I hope you have already started to do this – to look out for things for which you can be thankful. And now that you have started the habit, keep it up.

My Father, this is a habit I want to keep. Help me develop an eye that notices the good things of life and gives thanks for them. Amen.

GOD'S AGENTS OF BLESSING

FOR READING & MEDITATION – 1 TIMOTHY 2:1–11

I urge, then, first of all, that … thanksgiving
be made for everyone … (v 1)

One day a Methodist minister began to think of the blessings God had given him throughout his life. There came to mind the lady who had taught him in his first years at school. She had put a love of all things good in him, so he wrote her a letter of thanks. Written in a feeble script was the reply, 'My dear Willie, I cannot tell you how much your note meant to me. I am in my eighties, living alone in a small room, cooking my own meals, lonely, and lingering behind. You will be interested to know that I taught in school for forty years and yours is the first note of appreciation I ever received. It came on a cold blue morning and it cheered me as nothing has in many years.'

God likes to be thanked, and He likes his agents to be thanked also. Those with inner spiritual strength and poise will have a thankful heart.

O God, help me to be more sensitive and alert and thank those through whom your blessings have come into my life. In Jesus' Name. Amen.

ADJUSTING TO CHANGE

FOR READING & MEDITATION – REVELATION 22:1–6
On each side of the river stood the tree of life, bearing
twelve crops of fruit, yielding its fruit every month. (v 2)

The sixth principle we need to adopt is this: accept the fact of
change, and make out of every period of life something beautiful and good.

I have selected the verse at the top of this page as our text for
today because of the interesting thought that the tree of life, situated on each side of the river that flows through the city of God,
yielded its fruit every month.

The 'tree of life' in the here and now – our natural life – yields
its fruit every month also. By that I mean every stage of our life
– youth, middle age, and old age – yields something beautiful and
good. Someone has said that really there are just three stages:
youth, middle age, and 'You are looking very well!' Whatever our
age, we can always do something to make the time process beautiful. And it adds greatly to our spiritual poise and power if we
know how.

*O God, help me adjust to all of life's changes and to beautify
the hours, days, and months as they come and go. In Jesus' Name.
Amen.*

THEN GO ...

For reading & meditation – 1 Timothy 4:1–16

Don't let anyone look down on you because you are young,
but set an example for the believers ... (v 12)

Knowing how to make the time process beautiful contributes to
inner spiritual strength. But how do we go about it?

When I was young I was given three pieces of advice. (1) Find
a faith to live by. (2) Find a cause to serve. (3) Find a fellowship
in which your faith can be nourished and the cause can be served.
If you do not already have faith in Jesus Christ accept him now as
your Lord and Master. Then give yourself to a cause in which you
can work to help others. And enter the fellowship of the Church.

Recently I read about a young man who was learning to play
baseball. After hitting the ball he didn't know where to run! He
had no image of the baseball diamond in his mind. Take this as
your pattern: Christ, a cause, and a community. Once you have a
pattern you know what you want and where you want to go.
Then go.

 Heavenly Father, teach me more, I pray, of how to make the
time process beautiful. Save me from wasting time in useless regrets
or reaching for the moon. Amen.

GO, SELL, GIVE

For reading & meditation — Matthew 19:16–30
Jesus answered, 'If you want to be perfect, go,
sell your possessions and give to the poor ... ' (v 21)

Today we see Jesus telling a young man who wanted to find eternal life three things: 'Go, sell ... and give.' Perhaps the Lord has a similar message for you today.

Go: be willing to identify the things in your life that are preventing you being the young man or woman God wants you to be. Make a list of the things hindering your spiritual life.

Sell: get rid of whatever is preventing Christ being the Lord of your entire life. Take time to develop your spiritual drive through prayer, the reading of God's Word, and fellowship with other Christians.

Give: put others before yourself. God designed you to be an other-centred, not a self-centred being.

Don't be impatient if you can't change the world overnight. Be faithful in the small tasks and God will give you bigger ones. 'You have been trusty in charge of a small sum: I will put you in charge of a large sum' (Matt. 25:21 MOFFATT).

Father, help me be faithful in the small things so that I am eligible for bigger things. Build into my life good and godly principles, I pray. Amen.

WHO IS THE GREATEST?

FOR READING & MEDITATION – MATTHEW 23:1–12

The greatest among you will be your servant. (v 11)

For young people the idea of freedom has great appeal. Young people love challenging the older generation. But in relation to personal freedom we must remember that freedom is gained only through discipline.

Be careful that you don't throw off restraints simply because you think they curb your freedom. God's moral laws must be obeyed. You don't gain freedom from the police by breaking the law. When you commit an offence you will be arrested. Those who try to gain freedom by throwing off all restraint are free – free to get into trouble with God, themselves, and others.

One more thing: start every day in the right way and it is more likely to end well. In other words, begin the day with God. Make that a habit so that it does not have to be decided daily. Pray whether you feel like it or not. It may be a discipline at first, but I promise you it will turn to a delight.

🐾 *Father, I accept that youth is a critical stage of life. All I can offer is myself and my weakness. Amen.*

KEEP ON GROWING

FOR READING & MEDITATION – 2 PETER 3:1–18

But grow in the grace and knowledge of
our Lord and Saviour Jesus Christ. (v 18)

We think now how to make the time process beautiful in the
years of middle age.

A form of depression known as 'middle age depression' – not
due to a chemical imbalance – results from the feeling that one
may not have achieved through the years what one had hoped.

Accept the fact that your life is part of a bigger story and that
God's hand is at work bringing his purposes to pass. Some of your
goals might not have been in accordance with God's plans for
your life. Don't wallow in self-pity – a middle-age tendency. God is
at work to achieve his purposes in your life.

When you get to middle age watch your middle. One doctor
says, 'There are three great problems in middle age – baldness,
bifocals, and bulges.' Watch those bulges. Keep your mind active.
Enrol in courses that add richness to your life! You stopped growing physically when you reached adolescence, but you should
never stop growing spiritually.

*O Father, help me turn all my experiences into expression,
and pass on to others what You have taught me. In Jesus' Name.
Amen.*

UNCHANGED AND UNCHANGING

FOR READING & MEDITATION – HEBREWS 13:1–8

Keep your lives free from the love of money and be content with
what you have, because God has said, 'Never will I leave you ... (v 5)

We continue reflecting on the challenges and changes that
we need to adjust to in middle age. Those who are married
should guard against wandering affections. Many affairs are entered into by middle-aged people, more to prove something to
themselves. The problem is not that their spouse did not understand them, but that they did not understand themselves.

If you are heading for an affair, stop right now and think what
is driving you. It is almost certainly a basic insecurity that you are
trying to meet outside of God.

Guard also against the growing power that money has over you.
People in middle age can become worried about the subject of
money, but don't let these issues burden you. The God who has
cared for you will be there also in the days ahead. Don't be afraid of
this period, for in the midst of all its changes remember you are in
touch with Someone who never changes – the unchanging Christ.

*O great unchanging Christ, You have led me in my earlier
life and will also lead on into the future. Deepen my confidence
and trust in You. Amen.*

WHEN ARE WE OLD?

For reading & meditation – Psalm 92:1–15

The righteous … will still bear fruit in old age,
they will still stay fresh and green … (vv 12, 14)

Having explored some ideas concerning youth and middle age, we think now about how to adjust to the older years. However we define this stage, how do we adjust to the change of what are also known as the twilight years? First, if you have retired and you still have your health, don't stop working. The human personality is made for creativity, and when it ceases to create it creaks and cracks and crashes. You may not create as vigorously as you did before, but do something otherwise you will grow tired doing nothing. Involve yourself in some good cause in your church or community. Don't stop doing things. Create.

If you have lost a loved one, don't mourn endlessly. Many people spoil their lives by focusing for too long on what they have lost. They think they are showing loyalty to the one who has died, but really it is a form of self-pity. After you have mourned, move on.

O God, give me that inner beauty and spiritual glow that never fades. In Jesus' Name. Amen.

GROWING OLDER GRACEFULLY

FOR READING & MEDITATION – PSALM 1:1–6

But his delight is in the law of the LORD,
and on his law he meditates day and night. (v 2)

Many older people become irritable and cantankerous. Check on yourself to see if this is so. Be courageous enough to ask a friend or relative, 'Are there things about me that hurt you or concern you?' Also, develop your mind for as long as you can. We are told the mind never grows old. The brain grows old, but the mind can help prolong the power of the brain by refusing to sag. Read some portion of a good book each day. Engage in activities that compel your mind to function.

On the physical level, keep your body moving. Exercise regularly. Not strenuously, but regularly. And above all, fill your mind with thoughts from *the* book – the Bible. Nothing is more beautiful than to see an older person grow old gracefully, to come to maturity majestically. Constant companionship with Jesus Christ will help you do this. Grow older along with me, remembering that the best is yet to be.

🕊 *My Father and my God, I know that all life advances. Help me to adjust to all change knowing that the best is yet to be. In Jesus' Name. Amen.*

KEEP YOUR BALANCE

For reading & meditation — Mark 12:28–34
Love your neighbour as yourself. (v 31)

W e are to love our neighbour as ourselves.

What Jesus is saying in our text is that our concern for our own welfare is natural and should be matched by our concern for others. Don't we all like to have a good home, a happy home, a healthy home? Then seek that for others. Don't we all like to satisfy our hunger and thirst? Then be equally keen to feed those who are hungry but are unable to find food or feed themselves. In this verse Jesus is not commanding love, but presupposing it.

Everyone (unless they are psychologically maladjusted) desires what they think is right and good for them, and this universal trait becomes the rule by which our attitude to others is to be measured. The challenge is not to love ourselves – we already do that – but to have the same regard for others that we have for ourselves. Self-interest and other-interest are to balance.

🖎 *Father, may self-regard and other-regard be balanced as perfectly as possible. I need your help in achieving this. Thank You, my Father, that I can count on You. Amen.*

SELF-LOVE VERSUS LOVE OF SELF

FOR READING & MEDITATION – ROMANS 12:1–8

Do not think of yourself more highly than you ought,
but rather think of yourself with sober judgement … (v 3)

We must differentiate between self-love and love of self. How often have you heard one person say of another, 'He loves himself too much?' What they are referring to are the characteristics of conceit, narcissism, arrogance, or self-centredness in that individual. That is love of self – therefore unhealthy.

Self-love regards the self as important and in need of proper attention, but not all-important – therefore healthy. But what about people who seem not to have a healthy regard for themselves? They have been wounded and need the help of a counsellor.

Self-love can easily pass over into love of self. We must always be on our guard, as Scripture warns us in our text, so that we maintain the right balance. A question well worth considering as you go through the day is this: Is the love I have for myself a healthy self-love or an unhealthy love of self? If you think you are not an impartial judge, ask a friend.

 Help me, Lord, to evaluate myself and discover whether I am governed by self-love or love of self. I would be a healthy person. In Jesus' Name. Amen.

YOU ARE WHAT YOU THINK

FOR READING & MEDITATION – ROMANS 12:9–21
Love must be sincere. (v 9)

The regard you have for yourself is the result of what you *thought* others thought about you.

People with a strong sense of spiritual assurance and the 'something inside so strong' we have been talking about are people with a clear sense of identity; they have a healthy sense of self-love and are comfortable with themselves. They have a strong base from which they can give love to others, and so they love in a non-manipulative way. They regard others in the same way that they regard themselves, and what they desire for themselves they desire for others also; they give as much time and attention to the needs of others as they give to their own wants and desires.

If you don't have a healthy sense of self-love then you will give out love in order to get love back. Your love will have strings attached to it. But we can come to a balanced view of self-love if it has been blocked. Let's find out.

Father, hold me close as I face the challenge of being the person You want me to be. Lead on dear Father. I will follow. In Jesus' Name. Amen.

CRAZY FOR YOU

FOR READING & MEDITATION – 1 JOHN 4:7–21

This is love: not that we loved God, but that he loved us and
sent his Son as an atoning sacrifice for our sins. (v 10)

If you do not have a healthy sense of self-love, how do you go
about acquiring it? You must focus on the fact that Jesus Christ
has a love for you that is unconditional, perfect, and will never be
taken away.

But you will not be able to focus on that love or accept it unless
you are willing to forgive those who deprived you of love. Now
that is not easy, I know. With God's help, however, you can forgive. Say something like this to the Lord and mean it: 'Father, give
me the grace to forgive them in the same way that You have forgiven me – freely and fully.'

There can be no progress in developing a healthy self-love without forgiveness of those who may have failed you. Focus fully on
the love that God has for you. Inscribe our text for today on your
heart. Meditate on it. You are loved. God is crazy about you. He
really is.

O God, show me who and what I must forgive. I am willing,
please supply the power. Make this day an unforgettable one in my
spiritual calender. Amen.

'I LOOKED INTO YOUR EYES'

FOR READING & MEDITATION – JOHN 13:18–38

'A new command I give you: Love one another.
As I have loved you, so you must love one another.' (v 34)

I suppose few of us could put our hand on our heart and say that we love our neighbour in the same way that we love ourselves. Those who do have a deep inner poise because the more we love others the more beautiful we become in ourselves. Let us never forget that the pattern for our loving is Christ's loving: 'As I have loved you, so you must love one another.' How does Christ love? There are many aspects of Christ's love which we could think about, but permit me to focus on one that is often overlooked: *He loves us not only for what we are, but also for what we can be.*

With his help we too can love people in the same way. Love is creative. But what if the people we seek to love let us down? Then we still become more loving, for it is impossible to give out love without becoming a more loving person.

Staying spiritually strong

DECEMBER 28

O God my Father, help me love as Jesus loved so that as I love others they will see not me, but You in me. In Jesus' Name. Amen.

GENEROSITY THAT GENERATES

FOR READING & MEDITATION – MATTHEW 6:19–24

The eye is the lamp of the body. If your eyes are good,
your whole body will be full of light. (v 22)

The eye is our outlook on life, our whole way of looking at things, and when our eye is generous then our whole personality is illumined – lit up. 'The generous eye and the generous attitude,' says a famous preacher, 'are at the basis of all sound relationships, for no relationship can develop unless there is generosity on both sides.'

Jesus is our example in this as in everything. He was generous towards everyone – the poor, the dispossessed, the sinful, the unlovely. When He is allowed to generate his generosity within us, then we begin to see everything through his eyes. I shared this thought with a friend some time ago and, after pausing for a moment, he said, 'His generous eye saw in me what I couldn't see, and it has generated generosity in me towards others.' This comment is one of the most beautiful I have ever heard. And remember that the generous eye fills the whole body with light.

Heavenly Father, help me make generosity the basis of all my dealings with everyone I meet today. And not just today but every day. Amen.

THE MOST FAMOUS COLT

For reading & meditation – Luke 19:20–ww

As they were untying the colt, its owners asked them, 'Why are
you untying the colt?' 'The Lord needs it.' (vv 33–34)

We spend one more day reflecting on this important concept
of love operating as generosity.

Suppose the little boy who figures so prominently in the story of
the feeding of the five thousand had hidden his loaves and fish from
the disciples. He and the crowd would have missed out on one of
the most sensational miracles Jesus performed (see John 6:1–13).

From what we have been saying, I hope it is quite clear that
when we are generous with others, we ourselves are blessed. We
must not be generous in order that we might gain a blessing – that
would be putting self ahead of others. We must be generous because it is the right thing to do. Meanness ought not to characterise
the children of a God whose magnanimity and large-heartedness is
so wonderfully displayed both in Scripture and in creation. Be a
generous person and, as night follows day, your inner strength will
increase. Eventually you will be naturalised in generosity.

🕊 *Father, I am making the decision right now that my approach
will be one of generosity. Help me find the good, further the good,
and do good in everything. Amen.*

LIFE HOLDS NO SHIPWRECK

FOR READING & MEDITATION – ACTS 28:1–10

When this had happened, the rest of the sick
on the island came and were cured. (v 9)

Jesus had inner strength and poise, and He passed it on to his early disciples. Take Paul, for example. Not one word of self-pity when testifing before King Afrippa – pity only for those who did not share his inner composure. Paul's inner strength was also very evident when the ship on which he was sailing was about to be wrecked in a severe storm. Paul the prisoner took charge, gave the sailors orders, and saved himself and the whole company.

The inner poise and power that Jesus displayed was shared not only by Paul but by all His disciples. The Early Church was filled with men and women who had 'something inside so strong'. But can we share it in this age too? Is it for some and not for others?

With all my heart I say a divine reinforcement is available for all who yield everything they have to the Almighty. Life holds no shipwreck that need leave us a wreck.

Father, stay close to me and help me build into my life every one of the principles I have been considering. In Christ's Name. Amen.